WOMEN AND SOCIETY

WOMEN AND SOCIETY

Equality and Empowerment

Jyoti Mitra

KANISHKA PUBLISHERS, DISTRIBUTORS
NEW DELHI 110002

KANISHKA PUBLISHERS, DISTRIBUTORS
4697/5-21A, Ansari Road, Daryaganj
New Delhi -110 002
Phones : 2327 0497, 2328 8285
Fax : 011-2328 8285
E-mail : kanishka_publishing@yahoo.co.in

First Published-1997
Second Edition-2012

ISBN: 978-81-7391-163-0

PRINTED IN INDIA

Published by Madan Sachdeva for Kanishka Publishers, Distributors, 4697/5-21A, Ansari Road, Daryaganj, New Delhi-110 002, Typeset by Sunshine Graphics, Delhi, and Printed at Rajdhani Printers, Delhi.

Preface

We see a new woman in the making in India, despite having to agree with the assertion of the National Commission for Women that "even 45 years after independence women continue to be treated as a single largest group of backward citizens of India".

This is a contradiction that is inherent in a multi-levelled society riven by caste inequalities, regional disparities and a cultural diversity that draws sustenance from any point of time in a 500-years-old past. Not to speak of the influence of several religions with their different codes as they are applied to the status of women. Unfortunately, our constitution makers themselves fell a prey to those contradictions in two ways.

They guaranteed gender equality and justice in the preamble itself as well as in Articles 14, 15 and 16 with the emphasis on equality of men and women before law, prohibition of discrimination on 'ground of religion, race caste, sex or place of birth or any of them and equality of opportunity in matters of public employment.' But a study by EKATRA for SIDA/DCO quotes jurist Upendra Baxi as pointing out that the Constitution has implicitly accepted patriarchal assumption—as the world's largest and most eleboratcly writtcn constitution, it refers to women only six times, out of which five times they are referred to together with men or children and only once and that too in the context of maternity leave in Article 42 to women alone. The report also mentions former justice V.K. Krishna Iyer as saying that the gender bias is noticeable in that when inequality is abolished between men and women in many matters, the domestic sector is left trgically untouched.

The second contradiction lies in the fact that though the goal of uniform Civil code is enshrined in the Constitution as the ultimate reality with its principles of equal rights for men and women, the laws relating to marriage, divorce, adoption, inheritance and other factors were left to be governed by the five personal law codes of the five religious communities—the Hindus, Muslims Christians, Jews and Parsees.

Unveiled in June this year, the Maharashtra policy was finalised after in depth consultation with women's groups, activists and grassroots workers. Several of the discussions conveyed the importance the government attached to the initiative—a necessary signal for the State administration which will be implementing the policy.

The policy has identified six focus areas for immediate attention:

- Steps to eliminate violence against women;
- Ensuring equality both in the spirit and letter of law;
- Improving the economic status of women;
- Appropriate use of the media;
- Enhancing community participation in Government activities.

Detailed strategies for achieving these objectives have been spelt out, though some of them such as change in personal laws to enable joint property rights for wives, may not be workable.

Among the innovative steps envisaged to contain violence against women are identifying areas in metropolitan cities where atrocities against women are high and set up police stations headed by women there. Another is mobile *suraksha kendras* manned by women to patrol such areas in the night in the next five years, 25 per cent of the police stations are to be headed by women. Maharashtra also launched a scheme for destitute women under which they would get shelter and paid a modest stipend for one year while they are given vocational training to set them on their feet again. Each district is to have a *Mahila Kendra* that will provide counselling, legal aid and literacy training.

The articles and papers in the present compilation seek to profile the aspect of equality and empowerment of women, a cherished goal for long. The materials have been intended for students and scholars alike.

Editor

Contents

Contents

1

Women and Transnational Dimensions

> There is a huge variation in the size of the territorial units to which people are at present attached by ties of feeling which seem to them immutable; the sentiment-evoking area may be a village, a great city, a vast province, a river, a mountain-chain, a state, an empire. New areas of consciousness are generating at this very moment. A United Nations patriotism may perhaps become a commonplace to future generations.[1]

It is no new thing for people to be seeking modes of international co-operation, but perhaps no earlier generation has been oppressed by so great a sense of urgency in the quest. We are all ever closer to each other and our different national lives ever more intricately involved. It is impossible to shut ourselves safely and tranquilly within our national boundaries. The fortunate aspect of this world situation is that we can, if we will, be as quick and effective to help each other as to threaten. How to tilt the balance towards reciprocal goodwill, or at least respect, is a problem to which people of equal integrity and experience offer different solutions. Some see a world government as a prerequisite; others look to an expansion of federalism over a considerable period of time; others to the establishment of more and more international institutions for practical co-operation, that is, to a functional liking-up of the world.

The search for a pattern goes back for hundreds of years, but for us today the significant beginnings of universal co-operation can be traced to the late nineteenth century, with the formation of the International Telecommunications Union and the Universal Postal Union. These established modern world communications. Soon after the turn of the century the long series of efforts to construct a system of international justice culminated in the establishment of the Permanent Tribunal at The Hague in 1907. These world institutions survived two world wars.

After the first world war of 1914—18 the League of Nations was set up, an association of sovereign states, not a world state, without an army or even a police force. Women who were schoolgirls or young students at the time remember the tremendous force of idealism inspired by international hopes among the young. The League of Nations Union helped to educate people of all ages in the cause of peace. However the league could not prevent the second world war. Had it been nothing but an impractical dream? One proof that it was much more is that even before the second world war was ended the United Nations had begun to take shape. In fact there was no break, the league did not wind up its existence officially until 1946, when the United Nations had formulated its charter.

The determination to continue to search for peace and co-operation thus remained in being through the years of war and was reaffirmed in the Preamble to the Charter, where the peoples of the United Nations declared their intention:

> To save succeeding generations from the scourge of war, which twice in our lifetime has brought untold sorrow to mankind ... to practise tolerance and live together in peace with one another as good neighbours and to unite our strength to maintain international peace and security. ...

What hope is there that these ideals can be achieved? One ground for optimism is this fact that certain world institutions continued to function all through the years of total war. The League of Nations was not concerned solely with political organization and war does not nullify its social and economic achievements. Throughout the second world war some of the league's economic research went on and the Health Section and Opium Section continued to function. The International Labour Organization removed to Canada and continued its work from there. The Permanent Court of International Justice remained in being at The Hague.

This necessarily brief review shows that nations can and do contrive even in circumstances of the greatest difficulty, in a world torn apart by war, to keep in existence a network of international services in the cause of justice, health, learning and other supreme human values. One also calls to mind the war-time work of such a great international voluntary organization as the International Red Cross, the supreme example of co-operation for the relief of human suffering.

It has been suggested that we are wrong to attempt to construct peace chiefly on a political basis by widening the units of national interests and political loyalties, whether by federalism or the creation of a world state. What is more important is to decrease the significance of national boundaries, so that a frontier might be accepted as an administrative convenience only. The flow of people, goods and services would be less and less impeded. Above all there could be a free flow of ideas. In different ways, the Specialized Agencies and the commissions which work in relationship with the United Nations are directed to these ends. All three councils of the United Nations are important to women: the Security Council which is principally responsible for keeping the peace of nations, the Trusteeship Council which concerns itself with the welfare and progress of the peoples living in Trust Territories, and the Economic and Social Council which covers the whole field of international social and economic co-operation. This last council, assisted by its commissions and the Specialized Agencies, is the most important for our immediate consideration; how to interest women in international affairs and how to help them to find ways of influencing international conduct. Three of the chief Specialized Agencies are those concerned with food, health and education: the Food and

Agriculture Organization, the World Health Organization and the United Nations Educational, Scientific and Cultural Organization (Unesco).

Let us begin with one of the projects of the United Nations which should prove of interest to mothers: Unicef, the United Nations International Children's Emergency Fund, which began its work for children and pregnant and nursing mothers in 1946. It provides help and protection for millions of children all over the world. Governments desiring its help draw up schemes which are submitted to Unicef which consults with the World Health Organization upon their soundness and practicability. One great project has been to increase the milk supply in countries where it is inadequate for the needs of mothers and children, to improve the provisions for keeping it good, and to set up plant to dry it for winter use. On this scheme the technical advice and help of the Food and Agriculture Organization has also been obtained. Such schemes have been operated in Austria, Czechoslovakia, Finland, France, Greece, Italy, Malta, Poland, Yugoslavia, Israel, Persia, Brazil, Chile, Ecuador and Nicaragua. Nor has the benefit stopped at improved nutrition. A *Times* Special Correspondent (18 Feb. 1953) writes:

> The vast feeding programmes undertaken by Unicef have had a permanent and far-reaching effect on the mothers too, for when they bring their children to the maternal and child welfare centres, they become available for regular health checks, and their co-operation is secured for the development of public health programmes generally.

Taking part in a public health scheme is an essential part of fundamental education. Necessary as it is to combat illiteracy these other campaigns are at least as urgent. Some idea of international action to foster fundamental education may be obtained from one of the Unesco projects which has attracted worldwide attention among educationists. This is the fundamental education centre at Patzcuaro in Mexico, where students are given a 21 months training course, preparatory to becoming disseminators of fundamental education in their native countries. The students, both men and women, work in teams in villages scattered through this beautiful but impoverished land. Each student has been selected by his or her home country as a specialist in health, rural economy, domestic economy, recreation and the use of leisure, or education for social responsibility. They tackle illiteracy in due course but are concerned first with the spiritual and mental problems of a people living in an ancient culture which has survived into the modern world. They tackle also the practical difficulties created or aggravated by inadequate farming, irrigation and forestry methods. For this project Unesco co-operates with the Organization of American States, the Food and Agriculture Organization, the International Labour Organization, the World Health Organization, the Mexican and other governments. It should be emphasized that the Patzcuaro approach to community problems is a 'global' one. Women are well represented on the staff and make up a considerable proportion of the students; this is indispensable when teams of students go to work in villages and attempt to make contact with all aspects of community life.

Among the commissions established by the Economic and Social Council is the Commission on the Status of Women. This body is concerned with women's political rights, their educational opportunities, property rights, status in family law, and is prepared to give consideration to any problems brought to its attention by governments and other bodies which touch upon the political, social, economic, civil and educational status of women.

The two practical examples of the work of the United Nations and the Specialized Agencies given above may serve to indicate that there is a great deal in the international field which should interest women. The bibliography at the end of this booklet will provide the reader with a number of sources for obtaining fuller information.

The importance of the work of the United Nations is brought home to women in many countries by the United Nations associations of those countries. When a country has appointed a National Commission to Unesco which is fully representative of national educational interests and which maintains a two-way flow of ideas and information, the educational resources of Unesco can be channelled to that country. Where women's organizations are lively and conscious on the one hand of their members' needs and interests and on the other of the opportunities afforded by the Commission on the Status of Women, fruitful co-operation can result. There always has to be activity on both sides, in the nation and in the international organization.

What factors contribute towards making women conscious of international relationship? The value of foreign travel and meeting foreigners in their own country can be negligible unless the right people meet the right people in the right conditions. There can be no doubt for instance of the value of the great conferences held by the International Federation of University Women with its 31 national federations in the five continents and its membership of 142,000 women. The IFUW is another of the women's voluntary organizations with which we have so often been concerned in different contexts; here we see the international value of their work. Members of a National Federation are automatically members also of the IFUW. When travelling abroad they are provided with introductions to other national federations and are given the privileges of their club-houses which thus function also as international meeting places. The IFUW has been granted consultative status by the Economic and Social Council of the United Nations and concerns itself especially with questions to do with the status of women and with university problems. It has also since the war given help to individual university women refugees and other war victims. The British Federation dates from 1907 and the International Federation from 1920.

That is one valuable and well-established kind of meeting and travelling with women of other countries, where there is a common interest and a permanent international body to which nationals of different countries feel loyalty. The International Council of Women casts its net more widely, for the range of women's interests represented is very great; but here again there is a long-standing, co-ordinating body which brings women together in fellowship and loyalty. In describing the great international conferences of the ICW its chronicler makes an acute observation. She says that their conferences:

> are always held where there is a resident welcoming force, a part of themselves that is on its home ground; and in gatherings of women there is always the domestic interest. Men visiting other men in their homes gather honey; but not so much as women visiting other women. A woman's home is part of her vesture; it is also part of her local background; in both capacities the visitor finds it fruitful of interest in a hundred unexpected ways. Foreign travel and domestic visiting are alike living educational forces.[2]

These are a few of the many ways in which people come together. Religious, political, scientific and trade union conferences come to mind at once and many others. Trade fairs and national festivals and exhibitions exert another kind of attraction but on the whole draw fewer women than men. The great majority of women do not travel abroad nor are they likely to have a wide range of useful contacts with foreigners at home. For them the most important, vivid substitute for the face-to-face meeting is the film. Any film can be made to yield some interest by a teacher who knows something of its subject and is skilled in the discussion of films; but without such guidance the ordinary commercial films from a foreign country can be most misleading. Unesco as part of this work assists the production and interchange of films likely to further international understanding. For example, a film has now been made which shows the work of the United Nations and some of its Specialized Agencies. (The Patzcuaro Fundamental Education Centre referred to above is one of the projects shown.) The makers of the film hope that it will 'show vividly and imaginatively what is common to the problems and achievements of the United Nations in various lands widely separated.[3]

Most countries produce educational films and one of Unesco's projects is to establish a free flow of these films across national boundaries. One interesting exchange may be noted as an example;

the making of the film, *Mr. English at Home,* for use in Africa, to give as true a picture as possible of an ordinary English working-class home. This was made by the Colonial Film Unit which has also (and chiefly) been working since 1945 in Africa, producing films about Africans designed for Africans, but of great potential interest to English people too. It seems likely that in time many countries will produce films about their national ways of life and their achievements which are designed to be seen by the people of other countries and to foster understanding of the real people who live behind the mask of caricature that disguises nations from one another. Another interesting Unesco project in this field is a series of studies of the ideas which nations have of other nations and of themselves and of how they represent foreigners in the press and in films and radio.

Another approach, where there is no language barrier and where the people concerned are literate, is through the exchange of letters ('pen-friendships'). This need not be a communication between individuals, interesting and enjoyable though this can be; a women's club in one country can adopt a sister club elsewhere. Not only letters but photographs, log-books, newspapers and books and other gifts can be exchanged. Sometimes these group friendships lead to an exchange of visits when distance is not an insuperable barrier.

Finally, we must remember that as illiteracy dwindles it becomes more and more important what people read. The quality of the press of a country is of the greatest importance to citizenship. In countries where practically everybody can read, many read little except newspapers. Women are often allocated a page or a column for their special interests—clothes, cookery, child care and housekeeping. In far too many cases one suspects that they read little of the rest. Some of such women's sections are, however, outstanding contributions to popular education; without losing touch with these special feminine interests they widen them by bringing to their readers a constant flow of news about women's problems, activities and needs all over the world. An able and socially responsible woman journalist can be a great force among other women.

The reference to 'needs' may remind us that we began this brief account of women's international interests with the Unicef feeding scheme for children. It is probably true that among women the most effective appeal to interest, sympathy and co-operation is a call to help children and their mothers. There is constant flow of money and goods about the world, dispatched by men and women of goodwill to people and areas suffering want. This is the most obvious way in which ordinary people can help the cause of international goodwill. Where educational needs are concerned, Unesco helps to put those who wish to give directly into touch with those who are in need, through the Unesco gift coupon scheme. Organized groups (clubs or schools for example) can get a list of needy groups and their particular requirements and buy enough gift coupons to cover the cost of the project they have chosen. The donors send the gift coupons with a personal letter to the group whose needs they are helping to meet.

Another gesture of fellowship which appeals especially to young people is the international work camp where young people from many countries work together at hard, necessary tasks in an area with special needs. Teachers who train abroad or go on exchange to a foreign country are in an especially favourable position to promote understanding; so too are women delegates from government or the professions to international conferences. What about—once again—the ordinary woman?

It is no service to a cause to underestimate the difficulties in the way. We must look fairly and squarely at the giants that bestride the path to international understanding, goodwill and co-operation. First, ignorance, linked with frustration and making for prejudice and irrational hostility; secondly, what has been called the natural 'provincialism of the human mind', our tendency to restrict intellectual curiosity and sympathy to the not-too-distant object, human or otherwise; thirdly, laziness; fourthly, the need for a scapegoat, an inferior, an outsider—someone who will draw off hostility and contempt so that we can stay at peace with each other inside our own group and direct our disruptive tendencies outwards.

One thing which we need to get clear is that international 'understanding' and 'goodwill' and 'co-operation' are not interchangeable terms. We do not necessarily, in our daily lives, feel goodwill towards those whom we understand nor do we always co-operate effectively with people towards whom we feel goodwill. It is sentimental to suppose that people of different nationalities have only to be brought together to like each other, or that constructive activity in the international field will necessarily follow upon a series of illuminating and popular meetings on international affairs.

The international is the most difficult of the three concentric spheres of influence, for women as for men: local affairs are still closely related to the face-to-face group, intelligible, affecting ourselves and our own folk; national affairs are more complex, bigger, more remote and less intelligible, affecting people, however, whom we still feel to belong to us even if we do not know them personally and even if they speak another dialect and have different ways from those of our own family and locality; but with international affairs there is a change in quality as well as in quantity. The personal element becomes tenuous. The relationship is now between structures—governmental, non-governmental, intergovernmental and supragovernmental. Yet the web of personal relationships covers the world too and although it is thin-spun it is incalculably tough.

There are relationships primarily of chance, such for example as the kinship ties between branches of a family which have settled in different countries. There are others in which choice has a greater part, arising for example from the correspondence between members of the same profession or business in different countries; between members of a church with an international body of worshippers or between members of any voluntary association pursuing a common interest which overrides national barriers. There are also the innumerable relations which arise between chance-met individuals who choose to pursue each other's acquaintance. Chance and choice both play their part. Both, for instance, have had a share in getting this particular book written by its particular author and in putting it into the hands of its particular readers. Choice will enter in again if some readers write to the author offering her a share of their own experience and information or asking her for further explanation or information for themselves. There is a kind of openness to experience which is the antithesis of the 'natural provincialism of the human mind' and which all of us can, if we will, cultivate as being the most precious piece of our human equipment for living.

At the head of this chapter is a passage in which reference is made to 'new areas of consciousness ... germinating at this very moment'. We can think if we will of some women as growing-points in their nation. They are fully conscious of themselves as citizens of the world and they perceive the relation between the policy of their country towards the United Nations and the prospects for world peace. They are the leaders and teachers, if they accept the role, of other women. The majority of women do not understand these things. The women who do, have to press for the education of the others, but meantime a great responsibility rests with them to be spokesmen for the less articulate and to interpret their needs and wishes. In order to fulfil this task they must keep closely in touch with other women. One of the ways in which this can be brought about is by the creation and fostering of women's organizations of many kinds within which any woman can find a place and discover the strength which belongs to a union based upon mutual respect for differences and integrated by an honourable aim.

REFERENCES

1. William A. Robson, *op. cit.*, p. 108.
2. National Council of Women of Great Britain and Ireland, *op. cit.*, p. 30.
3. From a report in *The Times*.

2

Sociology of Women and Work

Measuring Women's Work

> There are ... two facets to a basic-needs strategy for women in developing countries. One is to enable them to contribute more effectively to the satisfaction of their families' basic needs, within the framework of their traditional responsibilities. The other, which is a fundamental need of the women themselves, is to ease their work burden while furthering their economic independence and their more equitable integration into the community, beyond the narrow circle of the family.
>
> Especially in the rural areas, most women in developing countries are overworked rather than underemployed, and a more appropriate technology for the tasks they perform implies labour saving, in order to improve the quality of their employment, rather than employment creation (ILO 1978 : 61).

Demographers are interested in work, or more narrowly in 'labour force participation' because it interacts with so many demographic variables. For both males and females there are strong causal links between both occupation and work status and marriage, fertility, migration and mortality (Youssef 1974; Kupinsky 1977; Hunt 1965; Jones and Lucas 1979; Retherford 1975). In order to understand the nature of these causal relationships it is necessary to have reliable data on the working behaviour of individuals.

There is also the practical factor that demographers work with censuses and almost all censuses, except the most limited, collect data on the economic characteristics of the population (ECA 1974a).

From the point of view of women and development, one of the biggest barriers preventing women from having adequate recognition and opportunities to participate in development is the acceptance of the myth that women do not work. Thus in Indonesia a Government statement explains that Indonesia faces a heavy dependency burden because it is only the men who work (50 per cent) and if the aged (10 per cent) and children (15 per cent) are subtracted this leaves only 25 per cent of the population to participate in development and to work to support the rest (*Angkatan Bersenjata* July 1973, quoted in Hull 1979). This perception of women 'not working' is reflected in the Indonesian Government's Family Welfare Education Programme which teaches rural women that they have five major duties as:

(i) Producers of the nation's future generation,
(ii) Wives and faithful companions to their husbands,
(iii) Mothers and educators of their children,
(iv) Managers of the household,
(v) Citizens (quoted in Hull 1979).

Thus, through lack of understanding of the roles which women actually play, rural women are presented with an inappropriate middle class urban and pronatalist model to copy. Usually women who serve the state by playing vital but humble roles in agriculture or factory production become heroines and models to be copied only in centrally planned economies such as Russia and China (Broyelle 1977). In Indonesia, the 1971 Census actually showed that formally defined participation rates varied from 20 per cent in the province where women are least visible to 48 per cent where they are most active.

According to Fong (1980) 'one reason that women are too easily excluded from national development planning is because they are victims of old fashioned statistics'. Thus, in Bangladesh the establishment of a single factory manufacturing nylon fishing nets threatened to displace some 10,000 unrecorded women who produced nets at home (D'Souza 1980). In Peru a vast dairy farm/factory rendered redundant countless women who engaged in dairying in their own houses (Deere 1979). In Jammu and Kashmir in India the UNDP supported a project to modernize the woollen handloom industry. Here increased male employment was counted as a gain but the loss of employment by women was not entered into the evaluation (Jain 1980). Because of inadequate data, planners fail to recognize that development projects are effectively robbing women to pay men as employment is taken away from unrecorded women in the informal sector and given to highly visible men working in the formal sector (D'Souza 1980).

The very idea of a strict separation between work and the rest of life developed during the industrialization of the West as the use of clocks and watches became widespread (Minge-Klevana 1980). Interest in the concept of the labour force developed in the United States during the depression when there was much concern to measure unemployment. Naturally the concepts used were designed for, and best suited to industrial economies where the majority of the population in the labour force is in stable wage employment and where almost all adults who are not in the labour force are students, housewives or pensioners (Standing 1978).

Applying these concepts to developing countries with large subsistence sectors was bound to prove difficult. In the case of men it was relatively simple to assume that any adult male who was neither a student nor an invalid was in the labour force even if only as an unpaid family worker. In the case of women the crucial issue revolved around being able to distinguish housewives from members of the labour force. Women who work for wages or men who worked on their own or their family land were clearly in the labour force, but what of wives who did some work on the family land or in the family business? 'The crucial point which arises and which appears to have been quietly ignored in the instructions issued in most censuses is whether the vast number of women who are periodically engaged in subsistence agriculture should be classified as economically active or not' (Blacker 1977). There is much disagreement as to how many hours per week or how many weeks per year women must contribute to the family enterprise before they can be counted as members of the labour force. This is evident in the definitions adopted in the Asian censuses described in Cho (1976). In one Fijian survey the dividing line revolved about the number of chickens: a wife who cared for nine chickens was classified as a housewife but a wife caring for ten or more chickens was recorded as an agricultural worker (WFS Fiji 1976).

A basic contradiction is that housework performed for one's own family is not counted as economic activity, unlike housework performed for an employer. It is increasingly being debated why there should be a need to distinguish between housewives and members of the labour force (United Nations 1977; Fong 1980). Estimates of the value of housewives' services in developed countries usually suggest that they are equivalent to approximately a quarter of the Gross National Product (Clark 1958; Gelber 1970). It is difficult to see why such a significant contribution should continue to remain unquantified ((Bangladesh Economic Association 1977).

It has been strongly argued that in developing countries variations in the proportion of women recorded as being in the labour force simply reflect variations in the classification of farmers' wives (Boserup 1975). Thus in Turkey and Thailand where most farmers' wives are included, the proportions of the total labour force which are female are 36 per cent and 39 per cent respectively. In Egypt and Bangladesh where only women in wage earning employment are counted the proportions are seven per cent and four per cent (ILO 1979). Since there is little variation in male participation rates it is the classification of women which determines both the proportion of the population which is recorded as economically active and the total size of the national labour force.

In the rural areas of many developing countries there is effectively little or no time for the housewife to herself. Most women spend little time on domestic work, such as cooking, cleaning and child care: most of their time is spent in providing the types of goods and services which are bought for money in industrialized countries, producing and processing food and providing fuel and water (Boserup 1975). 'In premodern societies, agricultural labour is domestic and there is no conflict between female labour and domesticity; the female farmer, the wife and the mother are one. When a working women must move into contact with non-kin, when she can no longer walk out of the back door and hoe corn, her work becomes problematic for her, her family, and the society' (Wilensky 1968).

Maximum participation rates for women have been recorded in Rwanda where 96 per cent of all adult women were included in 1970 (Lucas 1976), and in the 1891 United Kingdom Census where all adult daughters living at home and not otherwise classified were counted as domestic workers* (UK) Census 1904). It should be noted that Rwandan women manage to combine sole responsibility for growing the national staple food crop, beans, with a total fertility rate of 7.8 (U.S. Bureau of the Census 1979). Whilst farm wives are usually classified as unpaid family workers, the 1964 Botswana Census took the stand that women were partners in the family enterprise and thus classified them as self-employed.

Minimal participation rates are all found in Muslim countries where it is shameful for men to admit that their wives are anything other than housewives. Thus, in the Algerian Census of 1966 only 23,315 women were returned as agricultural workers, but official estimates were that some 1,200,000 women regularly involved in farm work were not reported as economically active (Durand 1975). In fact, during the 1966 Census the Algerian enumerators were specifically instructed not to record other activities for women who were also housewives. The result was that the percentage of all females in the economically active population apparently fell from 25 per cent in 1954 to two per cent in 1966 (Blacker 1977). Nassef (1970) has explained that women's

---

* Unless otherwise specified, participation rates in this chapter refer to the percentage of adult women who are officially defined as being in the labour force.

work in Egypt is not adequately reported because of the 'traditional line of thinking about women's role and ... discounting of the importance of their part in the work of the farm'. Thus the statistics often represent the ideal rather than the actuality, especially where the ideal teaches that for a woman 'having to work is an aberration in the same sense that unemployment is an aberration for a working male' (Banerjee 1979). In Upper Volta the official labour force participation rate for females over the age of 15 is three per cent. However the report of the 1975 Census, from which this figure is drawn, simply states that no way was found of measuring female activity rates despite women's 'intense' contribution to agriculture (Upper Volta 1978).

There is a natural tendency to believe that statistics which appear in print in reputable publications must have a firm basis in fact. However the figures which represented Kenyan labour force participation in the Kenyan Government's *Statistical Abstract* and the ILO's *Labour Force Estimates and Projections* (1974, are 'based on data concerning the Bantu population in the censuses of the Republic of South Africa and Namibia held between 1946 and 1960' (quoted by Anker and Knowles 1978).

Where statistics are based upon survey data collected locally there are still considerable problems in measuring labour force participation. In one Kenyan survey, heads of household were asked about the jobs and unemployment of each household member during the last twelve months while married females were asked about the work they had been doing since marriage. In urban areas (after excluding women who reported that they worked as 'housewives only') the figures obtained from the male household heads were very similar to those obtained from wives. However, in rural areas the women were more than twice as likely to report that they were engaged in farming as the male household heads (Anker and Knowles 1978).

Even in cultures where women are expected to work outside the home, as in coastal West Africa, hurried reporting by male household heads is likely to underestimate women's economic participation. Thus probing during the Post-Enumeration Survey which followed the 1960 Ghana Census showed that 45 per cent of the women who were recorded as home-makers in the Census were, in fact, gainfully employed (Blacker 1977).

Anthropologists have approached the measurement of women's participation from a different viewpoint: that of the overall sexual division of labour (Brown 1969 and 1970). This approach examines all the tasks which have to be carried out in a society and looks to see who actually carries out each task. This method has the advantage of recognising that childrearing and housework are essential services without which society would not survive. Many feminists have argued that all sexual inequalities are based on the sexual division of labour and that its abolition would result in overall equality between the sexes (Dixon 1976). This means not only that women participate equally in the public spheres of life but also that men participate equally in the private spheres. If men are equally involved in cooking, cleaning and childcare it is impossible for them to maintain an authoritarian stand as lords and masters (Rosaldo and Lamphere 1974).

Heath (1958) examined the sexual division of labour in subsistence production in 398 traditional societies for which there were anthropological data. In no society were women responsible for more than 80 per cent of subsistence production but in 27 per cent of the societies they were responsible for more than half of all subsistence production. Most commonly women were responsible for a third of production. In 6 per cent of the societies women were recorded as being responsible for none of the subsistence production. This was because tasks such as food processing and the making of cloth and clothing were excluded from the definition of subsistence production. Almost all traditional societies consider that the division of labour is enforced by nature, yet Murdock (1949) found that in a sample of 432 societies every task (excepts metalworking) that was carried out by men in one society was also carried out by women elsewhere (and *vice versa).*

More recent estimates, based upon actual time budget studies, rather than upon masculine comments, have increased the proportion of total food production allocated to women. Although there are wide variations between cultures, in traditional societies around the world women bring in, on average, some 30-40 per cent of food consumed (Coppinger and Rosenblatt 1969; Sanday 1973). For much of Tropical Africa women's contribution equals as much as 60 per cent of total production (ECA 1974b).

Changes in Women's Participation in the Labour Force During Economic Development

Given all the problems inherent in measuring women's labour force participation which have been discussed above, it is clearly very difficult to make valid comparisons between countries or over time. Some apparent trends are simply artefacts of the way in which women are classified. Thus in countries where almost all rural women are recorded as housewives, modernization and urbanization are certain to result in an increase in the levels of participation as some women move to the towns and secure jobs in the formal sector there.

Early writers, who were very conscious of what was happening in the towns, were certain that the labour force participation of women increases during socio-economic development (Patai 1969). They also thought that this paralleled nineteenth century European experience. However this historical view was a very narrow one which focused on the new experiences of middle class women who wrote about their own lives, and ignored poor women who had always had to find employment as factory hands, domestic servants and agricultural labourers. Similarly discussions of changes in Asia concentrated on the theory of purdah and the work of middle class liberal reformers rather than on poor women working in the fields (Omvedt 1979).

Despairing of adequate data on female participation in agriculture some more sophisticated analysts have limited their discussion to non-agricultural employment (Wilensky 1968; Youssef 1974). Thus Collver and Langlois's (1962) study shows that the relationship between the proportion of women in the labour force and the level of industrialization is much clearer when the agricultural labour force is excluded from the calculations and becomes neater still if domestic service is also excluded. Frejka (1971) restricted the analysis to women aged

20-24, but this confuses differences in the life cycle with differences in levels of development.

Boserup concentrated upon 'employment in the modern sector as a percentage of all persons of 15 years or more' (Boserup 1973). While the percentage of all adults in the modern sector ranges from five per cent in the least developed countries to 36 per cent in the most industrialized, the proportion of adult females in the modern sector ranges only from one per cent to 22 per cent with no developing country having more than nine per cent. The best measure of the cultural acceptability of women being economically active outside the home is provided by the proportions of women in trade and domestic service because these occupations are available at all levels of development. Countries with above average proportions of women in these occupations are in South East Asia or have Negro or South American Indian populations. Countries with below average numbers of women self-employed or in the service sector are Muslim and Hindu cultures (Boserup 1973).

Studies which examine trends in women's labour force participation at different levels of development by restricting the scope to certain types of employment can only provide partial answers to questions about changes in women's roles. Most studies of the total picture support the U-shaped hypothesis that women's participation falls in the early stages of economic development to rise again at a later stage (Durand 1975; Sinha 1965). The explanation appears to be that the shrinkage of agricultural and informal employment opportunities during the early stages of development places women at a disadvantage, especially as preference is given to men in employment in the formal sector. It may also be the case that rising male incomes result in a lesser pressure upon women to act as supplementary income earners, especially in cultures where the whole family loses status if the wife works outside the home. Women's participation rates supposedly rise again with the spread of female education and the rising demand for women's services in the tertiary sector. Evidence of the downward trend in women's participation is generally more convincing than that for the subsequent upward turn (Durand 1975).

Whilst the U-shaped curve describes a general pattern, there are many other factors which influence women's labour force participation. Some of these factors which have been discussed in a developing country context are outlined in Table 2.1. The most intensive survey of cultural differences is provided by Youssef's (1974) study of the reasons why women's labour force participation should be so much higher in Latin America than in the Middle East. Even in the developed countries there are clearly cultural differences in the acceptability of married women going out to work. Thus within Europe the percentage of the total population which is economically active ranges from 60-52 per cent amongst males but from 44-19 per cent amongst females (ILO 1979: Table 2.1).

One factor which has received surprisingly little attention is the influence of childrearing responsibilities upon women's participation. Although there have been many studies of the impact of workforce participation upon fertility there have been relatively few attempts to concentrate upon the inverse causal link and examine the impact of fertility and other characteristics upon workforce participation (but see Ware 1977; Fong 1974). Much clearly depends upon the cultural setting. In areas such as Kenya, where women's participation is readily accepted, it is possible to show that neither in rural or urban areas does fertility, nor the presence of children aged under five years, nor the availability of another female household member who could undertake childcare, make a significant difference in the probability of female participation (Anker and Knowles 1978). In areas where poverty or need are the major factors influencing participation it is often possible to demonstrate a positive association between fertility and the likelihood of women's participation (for Malaysia see Fong 1974; for Sierra Leone, Snyder 1974; for the Philippines, Rosenzweig 1976). At a broader level Friedl (1975) has argued that it is the subsistence activities of women which determine the spacing and rearing of children rather than *vice versa*. Thus it is argued that denying women an economic role outside the home is a direct contribution to high fertility.

Table 2.1

Factors Affecting the True Level of Women's Labour Force Participation

Factor	*Where Discussed*
1. The level of economic development	Wilensky 1968; Durand 1975; Huntington 1975.
2. The style of development	Raviwongse 1978; SIDA 1974; Lini 1976.
3. The infrastructure available	Hackenberg 1979b; Guha 1974.
4. Government policy concerning the employment of women	Salaff and Wong 1977; Croll 1978; Davin 1976.
5. Laws relating to the employment of women	Kinzer 1973.
6. The type of work available	Youssef 1974; Castillo 1976; Yoon 1977.
7. The structure of the family	Collver and Langlois, 1962; Salaff 1976a.
8. Cultural traditions concerning men's control over women	Youssef 1974; Tuckwell 1976.
9. Cultural traditions concerning women's economic roles and responsibilities	Fapohunda 1978; Michaelson and Goldschmidt 1971; Dixon 1976; Ware 1977; Beechey 1978; Shah 1975.
10. Fertility levels and cultural traditions influencing childrearing behaviour	Popkin and Sohon 1976; Kupinsky 1977; Anker and Knowles; 1978 Weller 1977; Fong 1976.
11. Child care availability	Adams and Winston 1980.
12. Cultural expectations as to the need for and nature of housework	Coulson *et. al.* 1975; Gardiner, 1975; Secombe 1973; Jayme-Ho 1976; Szalai 1972; Vanek 1974.
13. Women's property rights	Lucas 1975; ECA 1975.
14. Women's educational levels	Standing 1976.
15. Women's ages at marriage and opportunities to gain independent experience prior to marriage	Dixon 1979; Salaff 1976b; Fong 1974.
16. Migration behaviour	Jones and Lucas 1979; Hackenberg 1979a.
17. Women's access to technology	Schmink and Chaney 1976; Ward 1970; Hirashima 1977.

Although housewives undoubtedly make an economic contribution the problem is that both the quality and the quantity of the output could be greatly increased with more specialization. Grain processing is an excellent example of this. Thus it is argued that 'to create more paid jobs for women is the surest way simultaneously to raise their status, to reduce their drudgery, and to raise the national output' (Lewis 1955). 'It is open to men to debate whether economic progress is good for men or not, but for women to debate the desirability of economic growth is to debate whether women should have the chance to cease to be beasts of burden, and to join the human race' (Lewis 1955).

Female Participation and Male Unemployment

One argument is almost always raised in opposition to any scheme for promoting women's participation in the labour force and improving their access to cash incomes of their own. The claim is that while there are men who are unemployed or underemployed their needs must come first. The assumption is that men are the breadwinners and therefore that providing employment for men will serve to provide for the whole population through their family units. This ignores the fact that modernization is usually associated with breakdowns in the extended family and with an increasing proportion of female-headed households where a widow or a deserted wife has to support her children.

More basically the argument over employment for women *or* for men reflects a misunderstanding of the origins of unemployment and the nature of development. Unemployment results from an unequal distribution of resources. It is not a problem in rural areas with labour intensive farming methods where everyone has access to a reasonable plot of land. It becomes a problem in urban areas because the disparity between rural and urban incomes encourages constant rural-urban migration and makes it worthwhile for the educated unemployed to wait for suitable employment. Boserup (1970) has argued that encouraging the employment of women in urban areas would have the following advantages:

(i) It would slow down the rate of rural-urban migration. This would mean that:

(a) more of the enterprising men would stay in the rural areas and promote development there;

(b) less new infrastructure would be needed in the towns by employing women already resident in the towns and the labour force could be almost doubled without the need for any more homes, schools, and roads.

(ii) It would result in the nuclear family becoming a two-income unit. This would mean that:

(a) families would be better able to pay taxes for the provision of urban services;

(b) families would have some possibility of saving to build their own houses to replace slum dwellings etc.

(iii) It would encourage fertility control.

(iv) It would also reduce the dependency burden because urban wives would no longer be dependent and because women migrating to the towns would no longer lose their productive role upon migration.

Governmental reactions to such arguments are likely to be very mixed. Most Third World governments would like to be able to effect major reductions in the rate of rural-urban migration but their power to do so, even by such indirect means as promoting the employment of women in the cities, is often very limited. It is easier for the governments of centrally planned economies. China provides an excellent example of a country where rural-urban migration is strictly regulated and women's participation in the economy is almost as great as that of men in both the rural and the urban areas (Sidel 1972). Some highly traditional countries have very high proportions of women in agriculture and very low proportions of women in non-agricultural occupations. Zaire in 1955-57 had both the world's highest proportion of women amongst agricultural workers and the world's lowest proportion of women in other occupations (Durand 1975). Many Latin American countries have high proportions of women in non-agricultural occupations and very few women in agriculture. However, developing countries with high participation by women in both agricultural and non-agricultural spheres are almost all centrally planned economies. Yet even planned economies cannot always overcome cultural barriers. While China has had considerable success in incorporating women into the general workforce, Cuba has been much less successful (Croll 1979; Bengelsdorf and Hageman 1978).

Time Budgets

Time budget studies provide a clear picture of what women actually do during the waking hours of the day (Table 2.2). Although some studies rely on retrospective reports on the previous day, the best data comes from actual observation by an investigator who sits with a watch and a time-sheet and marks down each activity including cases where an individual is performing more than one task at a time such as weaving and minding the body. Obviously such research is extremely costly in terms of personnel and quality control and can only be carried out on relatively small samples.

The advantages of time budget studies for the examination of women's roles are that they:

(i) Dispel the myth that the only economically productive 'workers' are the members of the paid labour force.

(ii) Show the dual burdens weighing on women who are responsible for housework and subsistence production, or housework and wage labour etc.

(iii) Show the bottlenecks in production and the total number of person hours spent in carrying water, gathering firewood, and grinding grain which could be saved through the application of simple technological changes and very small scale development projects.

(iv) Show the extent to which there is a conflict between childrearing and alternative uses of time.

(v) Explore the issue of the economic contribution of children either through their own productive labour or by releasing adults for more productive work.

(vi) Show how much or how little time could be made available for income earning work, literacy classes, participation in communal development projects, etc.

Table 2.2

Time Budget Data from Village Studies, Adult Females and Males

Activity	*Hours per Day*							
	Bangladesh		*Indonesia*		*Melanesia*		*Malawi*	
	F	*M*	*F*	*M*	*F*	*M*	*F*	*M*
Animal care	.14	.53	1.3	0.1				
Crop Production	.28	2.26	1.9	2.7	4.3	2.4	2.6	2.3
Handicrafts	.28	.03	2.3	0.4			0.1	0.3
Tradings	.07	.98	0.8	1.6	0.2	0.4		
Wage Work	.49	2.26	0.1	1.4	0.0	0.1	0.1	1.6
Other Income	.20	.83	0.0	1.0				
Hut construction	.15	.15			0.2	0.3	0.2	1.5
Exchange labour			0.1	0.8	0.2	1.1	0.1	0.1
Income Earning (sub-total)	(1.61)	(7.04)	(6.5)	(8.0)	(4.9)	(4.4)	(3.1)	(5.8)
Rice Processing	1.29	.01						
Firewood	.36	.05	0.1	0.2				
Housework	2.01	1.14	1.0	0.1	0.9	0.5	3.1	0.2
Food Preparation	2.23	.03	2.7	0.1				
Childcare	.80	.05	1.0	0.3				
Home Production (sub-total)	(6.68)	(1.29)	(4.8)	(0.7)	(0.9)	(0.5)	(3.1)	(0.2)
Total Work	8.29	8.33	11.2	8.7	5.8	4.9	6.2	6.0

Source: Cain 1979: 14; White 1976: 275; Kirkpatrick 1978: 290; Clark 1975: 84.

In one adult education project in Upper Volta it was found that wells had to be dug, grain grinding mills had to be provided, and donkey carts had to be introduced for firewood carting before women had *time* to attend (Lavrencic 1979).

The disadvantages of time budget studies are that they are only a basis for informed action and not a substitute for actual projects, and that they are only rarely absorbed by those who have to make the decisions. There are also many technical problems associated with securing a representative sample which will cover all classes of the community and all seasonal and day-to-day variations.

One remarkable feature of the available time budget studies around the world is just how little time adult women spend in childcare (Khan and Bilques 1976; Kirkpatrick 1978). In reports which include a specific category for childcare this activity rarely occupies much more than 10 per cent of women's time. Where childcare is included in a more general category of domestic work it is usually clear that there is little scope for the expenditure of long periods of time on childcare (Table 2.2). There are three reasons for this pattern:

(i) Daughters of the house often spend more time on childcare than their mothers (White 1976; Weisner and Gallimore 1977).

(ii) An average figure disguises the greater expenditure of time by mothers who only have young children.

(iii) Childcare is usually not a very demanding activity and thus is generally combined with some productive activity which is recorded as the primary activity.

Quite clearly any mother with a working day similar to those represented in Table 2.2 who wished to cut back the demands on her time would look to reducing the time spent in food processing rather than seeking to limit the demands of childcare. High fertility may be an economic burden but it certainly does not impose very great burdens on women's time.

Although detailed time budget data provide an excellent method of demonstrating women's economic contribution, even when in purdah, the way in which women's activities are classified may still serve to downgrade their contribution. Thus one Bangladesh study classified men's work on their own land as 'productive' but excluded women's farm work (Farouk and Ali 1975; Abdullah and Zeidenstein 1978). A more common error is to ignore the economic importance of 'family expenditure saving works' which produce 'Z goods', such as the processing of food and fuel, the repair of equipment, and the making of clothes and bedding, which are services which would have to be paid for if not performed by members of the household (Hymer and Resnick 1969). In some Muslim societies the belief that women do not 'work' results in the decision simply to omit them from time budget studies altogether (Abdullah and Zeidenstein 1978; Simmons 1976).

In contrast to the Asian situation where such studies are still rare, African women have been well served by time budget studies which have acknowledged that rural women work as hard as, or harder than men (Cleave 1976; Farrington 1975; Schwartz 1971). However this has not always resulted in planning decisions which take women's existing burdens into account. Thus in Tanzania those planning the early settlement schemes thought that an eight hour day was enough for men but expected women to work eight hours in the fields in addition to fetching water, childcare and spending two hours daily in pounding corn, securing firewood, and their other domestic chores (Brain 1976). Equally in Kenya planners protested that women were behind the demand for rural water which the administrators saw 'as a consequence rather than a cause of development' (Carruthers 1970). The reduction of the high proportion of time which women spend in tasks such as fetching water which are essential to the maintenance of the household, unfortunately has low priority even where women's economic contribution is acknowledged, and an even lower priority where women are believed to be just housewives.

The links between women's time budgets and their demographic behaviour are less obvious than the links with participation in development but they are still important. Firstly, there is the debate as to whether economic participation will discourage women from having many children. The other side to this question is whether women have children because the children are of value in reducing their workloads since the young can be used to fetch and carry and take over domestic responsibilities (Lucas and Meyer 1980; Ware 1978). Secondly, there are the demographic links between the heavy work burdens borne by rural women and their desire to migrate to the facilities of the towns or their experience of morbidity and mortality because of heavy labour especially when pregnant (Schwartz 1971).

Women and Development Planning

In the conventional view, women are of interest to development planners because they persist in bearing many children and maintaining rapid population growth rates which are believed to be a major restraint upon the speed of economic development. Just as the demographic aspects of women's lives cannot be understood apart from the total context neither can women's contribution to development be evaluated apart from their demographic roles. This is admirably expressed in the principles established by the Indian Committee on the Status of Women (1974):

(i) that equality of women is necessary, not merely on the grounds of social justice, but as a basic condition of social, economic and political development of the nation;

(ii) that in order to release women from their dependent and unequal status, improvement of their employment opportunities and earning power has to be given the highest priority;

(iii) that society owes a special responsibility to women because of their childbearing function. Safe bearing and rearing of children is an obligation that has to be shared by the mother, the father and society;

(iv) that the contribution made by an active housewife to the running and management of the family should

be admitted as economically and socially productive and contributing to national savings and development;

(v) that marriage and motherhood should not become a disability in women's fulfilling their full and proper roles in the task of national development. Therefore, it is important that society, including women themselves, must accept their responsibility in this field;

(vi) that disabilities and inequalities imposed on women have to be seen in the total context of a society, where large sections of the population—male and female, adults and children—suffer under the oppression of an exploitative system. It is not possible to remove these inequalities for women only. Any policy or movement for the emancipation and development of women has to form a part of a total movement for removal of inequalities and oppressive social institutions, if the benefits and privileges won by such action are to be shared by the entire women population and not be monopolised by a small minority;

(vii) that if our society is to move in the direction of the goals (of equality) ... then special temporary measures will be necessary, to transform *de jure* into *de facto* equality.

Evidently this book cannot lay down detailed prescriptions for the fuller integration of women into planned development. As the preceding chapters should have made clear, this is an area where cultural differences are of great importance. A solution designed for Bangladesh would have to address problems not found in the Philippines and *vice versa*. Even within each country there are considerable variations especially between urban and rural areas (Gonzalez and Hollnsteiner 1976; Women for Women 1975). In addition, there are very few successful models to be followed (Croll 1979). Indeed, in many cases where the position of women has numerous admirable features, these are often disappearing from traditional societies under the pressures of economic development projects which follow Western models.

Reading the suggested list of basic texts will serve as an introduction to many of the proposed measures for improving the position of women. Approaching the problem from another direction, the Checklist for Participation of Women in Development Projects gives a step-by-step outline of how to ensure that women are integrated into general development projects.

The starting point of planning for women is to be able to state the needs, problems, activities and interests of women on the basis of a good data base which includes both quantitative and qualitative information. The Asian and Pacific Centre for Research on Women and Development has produced a volume of 'Notes on Data Collection with Special Reference to Women' which is an excellent 'Do-It-Yourself' manual for individuals and groups who want to take action into their own hands (APCWD 1980). This manual explains the methodologies to be used but also stresses the importance of the participation of the women being studied and the truth that research is chiefly of value where it is followed up by informed intervention.

Recently there has been increasing awareness that rural women have been much neglected and that their existing contributions and their views should be taken into account in the designing of development projects (Independent Commission on Development Issues 1980; Nelson 1979; Palmer 1979; UNDP 1980; Zeidenstein 1979). Unfortunately, the findings of the growing number of anthropological studies of the factors which define the position of women are not generally produced in a form which is accessible to development planners (Ardener 1979; Hochschild 1973; Rogers 1978; Tifflings 1978). Similarly the findings of demographic studies which take a broad view of women's roles have only a limited circulation among planners in general (Chaney 1973; Reining 1977). There is still a great need of more synopses combining the findings of anthropologists, demographers and sociologists and bringing forward the policy issues which planners should bear in mind if women are to participate fully in development.

Conclusion

It is fitting that a survey of women, demography and development should close with a chapter on women's work. Women have always worked and reared children—what has changed is the relative valuation placed upon these two activities. In traditional societies the crucial issues were the production of enough food and other goods to support the population, and the reproduction of sufficient numbers of persons to ensure the survival of the population in face of high levels of mortality. Women were most valued as the mothers of the next generation. As mortality has come under a degree of control some 77 per cent of the population of the developing world now lives in countries with official policies to reduce population growth rates through a matching control of fertility (Nortman and Hofstatter 1980). Women are thus now expected to concentrate upon quality rather than quantity in childrearing and this in turn implies that women's roles and contributions will change (Oppong and Haavio-Manilla 1979).

Women's lives are actually more radically transformed by demographic and developmental changes than men's lives are (Stycos 1977). Modernization essentially involves the expansion of the 'masculine' public domain at the expense of the 'feminine' private domain of the family. If women stay in their traditional sphere then their world will inevitably shrink around them as education is taken over by the school, home production is replaced by the products of the commercial farm, co-operative or factory, and even entertainment and politics cease to be family affairs. Although many traditionalists would like to think that women, enclosed within the private sphere of the family, could be isolated from change and modern influences, experience shows that it is impossible for a nation to march forward on one, masculine, leg. Either women participate in development or they act as a brake upon the rate of progress.

The World Conference of the United Nations Decade for Women held in Copenhagen in July 1980 provided an ideal opportunity for evaluating the current position of women* and the potential for governmental action in this area (United Nations 1980). The background papers included reports from the United Nations agencies (Unesco, WHO, ILO) on progress made in education, health and employment. National governments submitted reports on their perceptions of progress made or on projects which they felt to be models of their kind. And the whole conference discussed the World Programme of Action which devotes some two hundred paragraphs to outlining what should be done for women. Typically, the most heated debate was reserved for issues such as racism which are of equal interest to men and women. (The overall impression was that the lack of debate over specific measures related to women reflected a lack of governmental interest in the area. In this case, more opposition to individual items would have been a healthy sign of genuine concern. The ideological differences which did appear simply reflected general differences such as those between capitalist and planned economies. Women as such, still failed to gain the status of a political issue. No government in the world stands or falls on its treatment of women. The problem is rather that everyone is prepared to pay lip-service to the idea of improving the status of women, if not to devote scarce resources to this end. Another problem with the governmental conference (there was also a parallel meeting of representatives of non-governmental organizations) was that so many proposals were inevitably phrased in terms of governments helping women rather than in terms of women helping themselves.

All United Nations conferences are inevitably remote from the lives of the common people, but in this case the distance was further increased by the fact that governments are essentially masculine institutions even where they are represented by female spokespersons. The vital message from the Conference seemed to be that the advancement of women is only to a limited degree a governmental matter. The essential changes are those which

---

* It may be mentioned that the last UN World Conference on Women, held in Beijing, did not produce as effective a resolution as the 1980 meet.

must be made at the level of the individual and the family. Hence the crucial link between women, development and demography. Demography is basically concerned with changes that affect families and women's concern with development starts at the level of the family and expands from there. Fertility falls, not because governments take action, but because families decide to have fewer children. Similarly, progress for women can be facilitated by governments, but will only spread when there is change at the level of the family (contrast the experiences of China and India). The idea of development from the grass roots up needs to be matched by a commitment to economic and social structures which do not handicap women from the start at the level of the family.

3

Women's Identity and the Professional Life

The shifting of the work setting from home to the factory after the industrial revolution has changed the concept of work drastically. Earlier the whole family worked as one production unit and pursued a craft which has socially ranked and integrated with the social structure. Thus the basis for identification was family occupation and not individual position in the skill hierarchy of the organization. The removal of work setting from home had an adverse affect on the position of women. Firstly 'work' had come to be identified as something which is pursued outside the home. Secondly, work had come to be identified with specific of the economic system. The work of women at home which produced only use value and which was not remunerated in tangible terms and which was tied to the day to day household chores had come to be regarded as non-work and participation of women is grossly under reported, more so in underdeveloped countries with dual economies than in advanced Western countries. This is discussed in detail by Banaria (1981) in his article "conceptualizing the labour force the under estimation of women's economic activities".

Along with the emergence of an organizational culture there is also a change in the occupational hierarchy with some occupations attaining an identity of 'professions'—elite occupations'. In this paper we argue that even the process of professionalization, like the process of industrialization is not in favour of women. Professionalization is basically a process of increased control and power. In the process women, who are less powerful in the over all social organization, are relegated to positions which are devoid of power and control, if not through deliberate discrimination atleast by the existential exigencies of working women.

Let us very briefly consider the elements of a profession. They are occupations based on systematic pursuit of knowledge and skills. Unlike the other occupation they are distinguishable by their control over the production, distribution and consumption of service provided by them. The exclusiveness of a profession is maintained by stingent admission procedures, a long and highly specialised socialization process and by successfully causing lay interference and control by autonomy or self-regulation and monopoly over the market. These are achieved through political manipulation elite recognition and by successfully increasing the social distance between the client and the professional by a process of mystification which has both technological as well as cognitive basis. The members of professional groups are drawn mostly from upper class and dominant ethnic groups and are predominantly make in composition (Johnson: 1979).

There are two points of view from which the relationship between women and professions could be perceived. One is the position of women is full fledged professions—medicine, law, academics etc. Another is the semi-professions—like nursing, teaching, secretarial work etc., and their attempts at professionalization.

Firstly let us consider the career choices and patterns of women entering the full fledged professions, which are determined to a great extent by this position in the social structure. Silverstone (1980) observes that all women use contingency approach in the selection of their career. "The contingency approach implies that women chose occupations in which they see the greatest opportunities for flexibility in which they can respond to any contingency such as marriage, child birth and geographical mobility. To cite an example practically all over the world medicine and teaching attract more women than the other profession for they provide grater flexibility and are compatible with *(a)* the image of women as pentle and emotionally responsive and *(b)* the 'mother' role of women. There are doubts about women's capabilities in professional fields which are derived from the belief that the ray biological functions of women. Would place their commitment to child bearing and rearing to take precedence over the competing demands of the professional life. The demands of the elder-in-laws as well as the household chores, which are still considered as women's area of responsibility hamper the uninterrupted pursuit of career. Silverstone and Ward (1981) point out that the career pattern of women in different from that of a man. While for a man career progresses from education—training-work—retirement. The career of most women follows education—training—work—interruption—retraining—re-employment—retirement. Interruption is accounted by the inevitable period a women has to spend in child bearing and child rearing as well as the subordination of women's career to that of her husband and the consequent geographical mobility. Interruption may sometimes require long periods of retraining. Re-employment may also be difficult in the face of competition from fresh and younger batch of professionals. For those women who are involved is highly specialised areas such as microwaves in electronics and surgery in medicine mobility is limited, as it is difficult to find suitable employers everywhere and self employment is expensive in most cases. A compromise between the roles mean sacrificing one in-toto which is a waster of the investment made in the training process.

The contingency approach to career choice restricts women to certain spheres of professional activity and discourages aggressive pursuit of career in competitive spheres. An interesting case in lady doctors in India. There is one lady doctor for 10 male doctors. 50 per cent of the lady doctors who specialise do so in obstetrics/gynaecology as this combines the tradition of female birth attendants with the high status attached to western medicine. The other options are paediatrics anesthesiology, pathology and aderiology. Surgery is least preferred as women surgeons are accepted with difficulty and it is a men's world. (Joyce Lebra *et. al.*, 1984). Thus within a particular occupation women are relegated to specific spheres which are less prestigious or powerful. The sex stereotype reemerge as the occupational stereotypes. Men who are viewed as dominant independent and capable are also viewed as practising professions that reinforce such images. Women who are secondary in the family and who play supportive sustaining and conflict resolving roles are expected to play the same role in the work setting also.

As we 'have seen already women prefer to take up free-professions which allow private practice or independent work—like medicine, teaching, academics, law etc., than organizational or ascriptive professions. Organizational professions, as the name itself indicates are practised only within an organization for *e.g.*, management disciplines and administration. There is very limited scope for private consultancy. Career progress in these professions is dependent on organizational employment. The number of women entering civil services and management courses is still very limited and dropouts are also more (case studies by Joyce Lebra *et. al.).* The participation of women is much less in ascriptive professions for *e.g.*, military and police. In these professions the bureaucratic as well as the professional elements are maximized and the organization also happens to be the professional association. The career of the personnel is much more closely tied to the organization with no scope for alternate organization where the skills can be pursued to the same extent. These professions are formally banned to women. Though in India women are entering police service at higher level but they are only exceptions. Women who are working in professions such as engineering, scientific pursuit, architecture, accountancy etc., find it very difficult to challenge the male stereotypes. They are further constrained by the difficulties they face in socialising with the clients, colleagues and others, the need for their presence in the field and the demands made on their free time. They have to be extra-successful to gain recognition in their chosen field.

Now we dwell on semi-professions, which are at the bottom of the hierarchy. These occupations have limited technical and cognitive inputs. They have supportive functions to play and are subordinated to a dominant group or profession. The membership of these groups is dominated by the underprivileged sections—including women. The limited technical and cognitive basis does not allow for much mystification, the main source of control over the clients. Since they are sub-ordinated to a dominant profession their scope for self-regulation is also curtailed. Since they are low paid, non-glamorous and are an extension of services which were earlier provided at home the semi-professions find it difficult to obtain elite recognition and cannot act as power groups or pressure groups.

Rose Mary deem argues that in the process of professionalization of semi-professions women are pushed further down in the occupational hierarchy with a new group of professionals dominated by men and other privileged classes, emerging above them. Take for instance nursing. Nursing theme role ideals, the 'mother', the bedbid psychiatrist and the administrator. While ANMS who emphasise the motherly role and are mostly women are considered as semi-professionals the nursing superintendent and such others who emphasize the other two roles, who are predominantly male are given a higher professional status. Deem says that men take ones an occupation when the technical base of the occupation is improving and the bargaining power of the group is better in the organization. There would be greate militancy and higher degree of professionalism at this stage.

Another aspect to which I would like to draw your attention is the general conclusion drawn by many studies that women are less professional in their orientation than men. Thus is so because the indicators are not selected properly in most cases with far greater emphasis on professional meetings attended, number of journal prescribed, research papers published etc., which show men who pursue their career mindedly is a better light than women. Sufficient emphasis should be placed instead on service-orientation. Commitment to tasks, effect put into the work and professional—client relationship etc., which would provide a more balanced insight into the professionalism of men and women.

Since the occupational hierarchy is a reflection of the social hierarchy. No drastic changes can be expected until there are far reaching changes in the society in its technological basis, value-orientations, power relations as well as division of responsibility at home. The fact that women are entering elite occupations in no cause for complacency until we realize and make conscious attempts to remove the inherent prejudices as well as the hindering social-structural imbalances.

4

Women and Development Mainstream

A. Criteria of Definition: The Context

From the outset, a definition of the integration of women in development is needed. Our definition is multi-faceted and includes at least six criteria as outlined below. It can be argued that the term "Integration of women in development" is "untenable" because women are very much at the centre of development. The term "recognition of women's contribution to development" would be better, or "recognizing women in development". To the extent that women are part of the population in areas affected by development projects, they have *always* been "integrated." Projects have negative and positive effects on women. The six criteria in our definition of integration for the purposes of this framework are as follows:

(i) In the transition from subsistence and reproductive activities to income generating ones women obtain an equitable share of the benefits.

(ii) Their particular role in the household economy in the reproduction and maintenance of human capital has to be recognized. These activities are often viewed as economic functions essential for the preservation and development of the family's and nation's human capital. Therefore, integration also implies improving

the visibility of women's productive activities by the timely collection of data on formerly "hidden" areas to bring out the contribution of "subsistence work, home production and market production..." (This contribution has been found to the equivalent of 40 per cent of total household income in some low-income households.)

(iii) Integration means that *all women's productive roles* will be considered in the design stage with an understanding of the implications for the implementation of projects. Socio-cultural and institutional practices in regard to the ownership of property and/or access to land and related resources, credit and technology must be included at an early stage in project design order to understand the interaction between project objectives and these practices, *i.e.*, an appraisal of possible chain of events set in motion by project activities.

(iv) There should be a *wident of choices* and women should have the possibility of making those choices. There are frequent findings in development literature that "... the process of change towards some type of capitalistic industrial society is .... detrimental to the .... politico-economic position of the women in rural areas". In the shift from an economy with an occupational structure mainly in the agricultural sector to one with industrial sector occupations, women should have opportunities for employment in the industrial sector.

(v) Integration also means facilitating the shift from subsitence to commercial agriculture which is especially difficult for women. Supports should be provided to help them make this transition *e.g.*, training access credit, price supports for their produce etc.

(vi) Furthermore, in both rural and urban settings, women should control their earnings, have the right to challenge the status quo, receive needed information which should be made available.

B. Assumptions

One of the basic assumptions of this framework is that the inclusion of women in development is not only a question of equality but also a necessity. Waste, be it rooted in social discrimination or economic irrationality, is certainly not the intention of development planners. However, waste will be the product of development projects which do not consider sufficiently this aspect.

Another basic assumption is that an understanding of how social, cultural, governmental, as well as economic and technical factors are linked is essential for a discussion of policy options and project design. A corollary to this assumption is that in development studies of this kind, we are dealing with "cumulative causation", *i.e.*, sequences of social and economic changes whose links need to be investigated.

Projects may be labelled as to their nature: economic or social, directly productive or non-directly productive. Imboden has clarified the matter by stating "The concepts of directly productive and non-directly productive projects are more accurate than economic or social projects." However, it has long been recognized that social projects are not irrelevant to economic growth.

C. The Project Approach

The project cycle starts with the identification of particular areas for intervention. Some donors have programme countries and concentration areas in each. The areas of intervention may or may not be those which have the greatest impact on improving women's participation in development, but their own reasons or perceptions may determine their choice. It is a moot question who initiates the project cycle and the selection of specific modes of intervention but advocacy and legitimisation of an idea do play a role. "Mandatory" integration of women in development began (for US AID) with the Percy Amendment (1973) and advocacy gained momentum after the 1975 Mexico UN/WID Conference.

Donors are often aware that cultural differences exist, but ignorance of how the situation of women is related to project objectives and fear of treading on the recipient's prerogatives are responsible for the neglect of women in project design.

For example, in one integrated rural development project in Western Asia in an area characterized by rather high male outmigration and where people's participation was a key concept in project implementation, no specific attention was focused, initially, on the roles and functions of women in the area. The host government made no formal request to include women in project design and at first this idea was greeted with some hesitation by the expatriates on the project team and by those employed in the Ministry of Foreign Affairs in the donor country. It was feared that paying specific attention to women would be viewed by the local people as an interference with the prevailing cultural values.

In the necessary interplay between respect for indigenous cultural values and the change to be brought about by action programmes envisaged, bilateral and international donors can play a crucial role. In order to play this positive role in integrating women into development projects, donors will have to change the assumptions on which their project objectives are based. "Conventional economics views the household as a homogeneous unit in which resources and income are shared equally by all family members. Available evidence, however, suggests that intrahousehold distribution of resources and income vary by age and sex ....". There are also differences in the way women use available resources. Most of women's expenditures go back into the household for food, cooking utensils, clothing and children's school expenses. Men, in contrast, with access to increased income are more likely to spend it on bicycles, watches, transistor radios and the like even if their wives are in dire need of an extra pot to cut down cooking time for meals, as shown by Palmer in her case study and a number of others. The same phenomenon has been found in India.

Knowledge of how this focus on women has reaped benefits in other projects can "fortify" the adoption of a women-oriented approach. For example, in a World Bank urban development project in El Salvador to increase women's demand for formal credit, review of the project showed that the credit component was very successful. As a result of credit to women family incomes have risen between 15 and 100 per cent, averaging around 35 to 40 per cent where the design had assumed an increase of only 10 per cent. Family welfare has improved on the whole, as women have become less dependent on the infrequent contributions of male members of the house-holds.

It was found for Bangladesh that the "... repayment rate of women participating in a rural development programme in Bangladesh which requires no collateral has been excellent. With two exceptions all loans due have been fully repaid."

The identification stage offers the opportunity to establish at the outset of a project whether particular enabling components, or pre-conditions, for women's successful integration should be included; and whether they should be in the form of separate women's projects or can merely be included as affirmative efforts within a general design. Too often problem identification is summarized in one sentence, without caveats which identify contingent problems. This is a deficiency for reasons other than women's concerns (for instance, problems posed by socio-economic stratification), but a reformulation of the identification procedure can bring out the fact that problems sometimes are seen differently by men and women.

In the project implementation phase if the necessary, "... information is unavailable or unsatisfactory, short-term, highly focused field assessments can be undertaken using case study approach."

D. Heightening the Visibility of Women Throughout the Project Cycle

Linked to each project category is the question of the target designation of group and the project cycle. Certain questions must be asked about the actors, the beneficiaries, the locus of the activity, the technology employed and the time dimension at each stage of the project cycle namely: identification, preparation, appraisal, negotiations, implementation and supervision and evaluation.

Projects which focus on activities in which women often predominate such as small-scale enterprises, subsistence food production or trading and agro-processing are more likely to include women in project design since the project's objectives and women's productive activities converge. This contribution is particularly the case when the lowest income groups are the project's direct beneficiaries since women's economic participation increasing with increasing poverty as Buvinic and Nieves document in their paper on the economic integration of women. However, it is especially important to identify women as target groups in general aid projects where they may not be explicitly mentioned and therefore forgotten.

Co-ordinated programmes which attack development problems from several angles simultaneously may be necessary and more effective. Such programmes must include measures of different kinds addressed to different sub-groups in the population. In co-ordinated programmes each type of project can have a catalytic effect on the others. For example, given sexual segregation in occupational roles in many developing countries, women-specific training projects may have to be envisaged, but these projects need not suffer from the usual weakness of focusing exclusively on women's domestic functions. The training provided should improve the earning power of these women and integrate them in the efforts to modernise the rural economy.

Women are not one monolithic block. Young single or married women are to be distinguished from older married women, as should the kinds of occupations they have or should be trained for in the family and village economy.

Project preparation which heightens the visibility of women's economic activities, *i.e.*, provides information about the nature and location of women's work, will help project management in implementation. In other words, an assessment will be possible of the extent to which women's productive activities converge with the project's production objectives. "... low visibility tends to be an important characteristic of poor women's economic behaviour". This is one reason why project design features will have to focus early, on the identification of target groups to be addressed, *i.e.*, matching the project objectives with the collection of data and an analysis of the needs of the sub-groups in the population, not just according to sex out by age, class and ethnic affiliation.

With a continuum of low to high visibility in mind, data will have to be collected in regard to family/household composition and the intra-household sexual division of labour with regard to the activities proposed. Available sociological and anthropological studies for the specific culture and region can be drawn on to provide an informed understanding of the traditional family/household economy and access to wages and other resources in the projects area. After identification of the target groups and the preparation of this data, an appraisal of expected project impact can be made in relation to this knowledge. When aid officials have been made aware of the importance of this kind of information it can be integrated into the negotiation stage of the project.

Data collection on the target groups to be addressed should always accompany design regardless of the project type, to make sure that the possibility of including women is always present. In some cases, "Designing separate women's components may be neither desirable nor effective; it may prevent women participants from benefiting from project components that are not sex-specific (generally those that are designed to increase productivity and income), or it may result in a duplication of efforts and an inefficient use of resources during the implementation stage."

In the supervision stage of a project, the foregoing point in the cycle will indicate the "specificity of the information required to adequately monitor women's inclusion in project components". This need for detailed data and more "finely-tuned indicators" should be reflected in supervision reports.

The findings of the evaluation stage can be fed into new projects as suggested above to modify project activities all along the project cycle. The main problem is asking the proper questions to help analyses what is needed at each stage.

E. Crucial Importance of Project Identification

There are number of explanations for the neglect of women at the identification stage of a project:

- Ideological bias;
- lack of base—line information about project participants and beneficiaries;
- administrative convenience in assuming that beneficiaries are a homogeneous group;
- assumption that all members of a family (men, women and children) will benefit from a project.

The following statement made by one aid administrator in relation to a project in Western Kenya indicates ideological bias:

> "As land ownership and the desire to utilize land for cash cropping becomes more important in the African areas, it is believed men will assume an increasingly more responsible role in the actual day-to-day operations of the farm. Thus farm women will have an opportunity to spend more time with the care of their children and home"

It reflect a common assumption among aid administrations that women in developing countries are prototypes of the "farm wives" in their own countries.

Another explanation of ideological bias against women is the view that men are the "primary foundation for agricultural modernization" although the predominance and expertise of women in agriculture is recognized. During the 1950s, the 'progressive farmer' strategy took hold ...". The goal of this strategy was to supply innovative farmers with inputs which would improve their productivity including tittle to land on which to do so. Land was registered primarily in men's favour. After a brief experiment with "out-reach" (special efforts to reach women) women were again invisible in agricultural policy strategies.

Ideological bias leads to a lack of consideration of necessary baseline information on the social organization of production, the sexual division of labour with regard to the crops cultivated and in the organization and staffing of extension services.

The multiple roles of women are not taken into account with this kind of bias. Instead of helping them to assume their various responsibilities it tends to "segregate" women into one of these roles.

The examples from the literature and projects considered in this review presented below indicate what women have lost in terms of their traditional access to land and other resources due to ideological bias and lack of baseline information. *When women are not explicitly included in the target population for project activities, implicit exclusion has been the result.* This is often due to stereotyped views and assumptions about the appropriateness of certain activities for women. Cultural perceptions and definitions of feminine appropriate work will influence the selection of the target populations.

Identifying the actors, the beneficiaries, the locus, the technology and the time dimension very early in the project cycle even without assurance of success in implementation at least makes the project management aware of the essential components and the necessary preparation

Because general aid projects are not designed particularly with women in mind, project management should be trained to avoid a uni-disciplinary analysis which does not encompass the possible ramifications of such projects. For example, the interaction between a whole constellation of socio-cultural, technical and economic factors would clearly have to be taken into account in a project to increase food production.

F. Distortions Resulting from Ideological Bias

It has already been mentioned how preconceived ideas, *i.e.*, ideological bias, adversely affect the integration of women at the stage of project identification. As a result, women have/no or reduced access to land and other resources and suffer from project design and implementation which disregards their roles. Experience of this kind is briefly reviewed below:

(a) Access to Land and other Resources in Integrated Rural Development and Resettlement Projects

Evidence of the negative impacts of projects in West Africa (in the mid-1970's) is provided by Bisilliat. The pattern that usually emerges is one of diminished access to land and other resources in the resettlement areas. Women traditionally had usufructory rights over their husband's land and also owned small animals such as chickens, goats and sheep. The latter form of mobile property is very important given their lack of titles to property of their own. Market activities were also important, covering products such as beer from millet, fried pastries, cookies or beans, condiments and nut butter. Artisanal activities such as cotton spinning to clothe family members, pottery and basket production for home and commercial use are other examples of traditional resources.

Women in almost all of these societies have certain family responsibilities for which they need their own resources: provision of food for family meals, gifts for baptisms or marriages, funerals and visits to relatives.

In one example (Burkina Faso, formerly Upper Volta) the programme of production established by the resettlement authority imposed intense agricultural work for men and women for ten months of the year. Therefore, the women's work load as non-paid labour was greatly increased, with less time to devote their other income generating activities.

Parallel to this increase in their unremunerated workload, women were deprived of fields on which to cultivate condiments, important nutritious components of the family diet. In the new development projects land was not available to women either on the basis of customary usage or according to the new modes of attributing land. Each family received only one hectare of village land on which to construct its dwelling and arable land of about one hectare according to the number of "active" family members who worked on the commercial food crops. Women found themselves completely deprived of personal agricultural resources.

Given the importance of personal resources, for the financial and nutritional well-being of families, certain women managed to get their husbands to let them use a plot of land but this was usually village land without great arable potential.

Market infrastructure was also lacking in the resettlement areas thus depriving women of at least 50 per cent of their economic power. To make matters worse, water and fuelwood were further away than in their former villages. It goes without saying that this work load excluded the possibility of attending health education or literacy classes. Initially no investment in wells or grain mills has been planned to lighten their burden.

In Senegal, the Cattle Development Corporation's project in the forest-pastoral zone in Ferlo (SODESP) could be considered a success in terms of the increase in income for those groups included. However, from the point of view of women it was a failure because the Corporation would not deal with anyone but the (male) head of enterprise. This excluded anyone with traditional rights such as women. Women who used to reap the benefits from the sale of milk were deprived of this possibility because the milk is now reserved for calves; and furthermore they no longer have as in the past a right to a certain part of the cattle which they had acquired through bride compensation.

(b) African Rice Farming

The research done by J. Day and reported in her 1983 paper, includes West and East Africa; it focuses on land and other issues involved in African rice farming systems. Dey has investigated the impact of 11 projects on women, which were developed under similar cultivation conditions but with different forms of development intervention. Her findings in relation to access to land and resources are reported below:

Governments were trying to increase food production and starting in the 1960s and 1970s they did this with capital-intensive and most often large-scale irrigated rice development schemes.

More recently and since the 1970s, a number of governments have focused on developing upland and swamp rice.

Five types of interrelated bias are most prevalent in the projects reviewed by Day:

- lost of land rights;
- technology introduced ignored the experience of women rice growers;
- technology introduced increased women's work load;
- family farm concept gave the male household head control of female labour;
- inputs, marketing and services were channelled through men.

5

Aspects of Women in Business

Passivism to Activism

During the transition from agriculture to industry and the ensuing social changes, there was no significant change in the attitude of women towards themselves, and their socially conditioned secondary position in the society.

During the first half of the twentieth century, while there were individual cases of women making strides in specific areas, as a group they made no real gains. Of course, in 1920, the nineteenth amendment had granted women the right to vote, but few used it.

After World War II, a number of women again remained in the labour force, and by 1958 women in managerial positions were not so uncommon. Margaret Cussler wrote in 1958 about the woman executive (manager):

> "The women executives studied have risen by finding a sponsor, by working hard, by taking what comes, and often by a haven in the women's occupations. They have rarely forced the issue. Only in exceptionai cases, often where they have started or inherited the business are women executives in the top job."[1]

The statement indicates little change still in the passive attitude of women in business to the time of its writing.

With regard to the future for women in the labour force, she felt that they could now sit back and wait for better jobs to come, from there happy, serene, and content positions. Of equal opportunity for women in the labour force, Cussler off-handedly said: "Many will fight for the right who do not intend or wish to use it. It is something to know you can, if you should happen to want to."[2]

This last comment, again indicates the thinking that women work out of choice, rather than out of any economic or psychological need.

Cussler's writing also indicated that women could expect advancement into higher management levels when the next sweeping changes occurred. There is no reference as to where these changes were to come from, but little indication is given that women themselves would have a great deal to do with their cause.[3]

In 1961, Francis Maule, writing about the future of women's role in business (as an executive/manager), claimed the only people, holding women in business from reaching managerial levels, were women themselves. While Maule, like Cussler, did not advocate the role of militancy, she did promote the concept that the opportunity was there, and you must go out and get it. This was a departure from the passiveness that had marked the history of women in the labour force until this time, as evidenced by Cussler's writing just three years previously. Maule's instructions of would be management women included the concentration of their efforts on their work, the acquisition of additional education and training, and the intentional development of the necessary behaviour patterns required of a potential member of management.[4]

While Maule wrote just prior to the legislation deemed so important, by many, she interestingly did not dwell in any great detail upon the need for outside assistance, legislative or otherwise, but stressed the need for women to actively pursue success in business if they choose to.

Over the ten year period from 1960 to 1970, the idea of an active role for women in changing their own condition became an accepted fact; at least to other women. One very vocal women's rights group representative of this new found activism was The National Organization for Women (NOW).

By 1970, NOW had become dissatisfied with the progress, or lack of it, which women had made, in spite of the recent wave of legislative effort. In a press release issued in 1970, an example of the active, multifrontal attack on the problems of inequality for women in society can be seen. By attacking the basis for the inequality, NOW was typical of the effort to better conditions for the working women, by attempting to change the causes rather than the results.

A list of the topics dealt with in the press release will show the scope of changes which were considered directly necessary to give the working women equality in the labour force, included:

Need for child care facilities;

Abortion reform;

Political role in the creation of legislation;

Equal Rights Amendment or similar broad legislation;

Aides built into the system, for women with complaints needing an avenue to direct them;

Equality of marital partnership, due to its effect on society as a whole in alleviating social role stereotypes;

Use of the media to rouse consciousness;

Challenge to the National Council of Churches, to aid in the equality movement, as they had aided in discrimination encouragement;

Promotion of female studies and courses, and the elimination of sex-role stereo-types in texts;

Equal access to employee training programmes, especially management development;

Supporting women for positions of political power.[5]

The response of employers to groups such as NOW, had been and continues to be one of outward non-concern; but, considering the tenacity and growth of such activist groups and the awareness they have created, this cannot be the true management response. Groups such as NOW are affecting the business world with external as well as internal pressures.

Another more recent response to the problems faced by women workers, being promoted by various women's organizations, is the concept of unionization. As discussed earlier in this report, the early women's work force in industry did not possess the necessary conditions for unions to succeed in organizing them. Women workers of the time also did not have the necessary desire to go through the pains of organization.

According to recent activity, the elements necessary for successful unionization appear to be present in today's working women. The move toward unionization in the offices is occurring, with "secretaries, typists, clerks, and other white collar women banding together, to overcome their low status and low pay."[6]

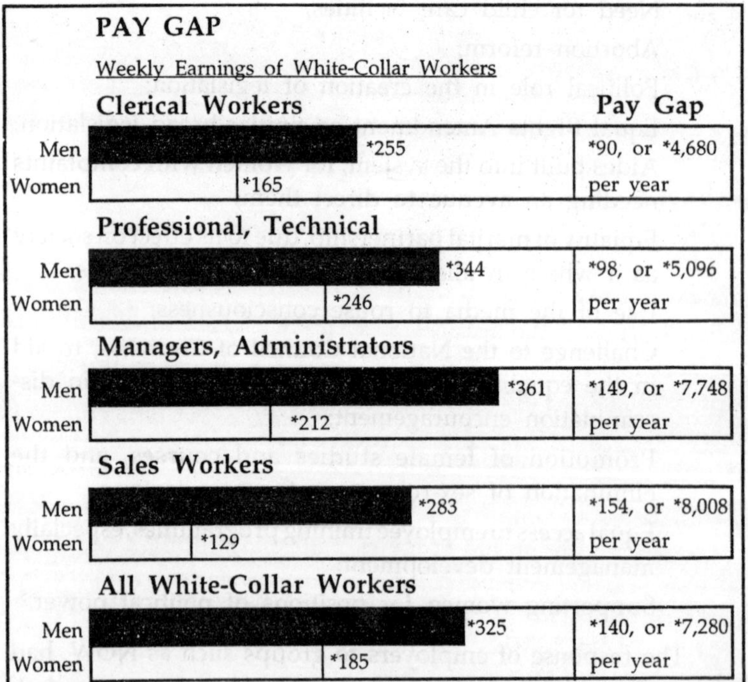

Note: Based on a survey of 56,000 households in May, 1978. Figures are medians—half named more half earned less.

Source: U.S. Bureau of Labour Statistics.

The chart[7] below illustrates the obvious inequality of pay between male and female workers, which has economically pushed this unionization movement forward.

Elizabeth Koontz, leader of the National Commission on Working Women, recently said, "Traditionally women have been judged by their measurements. Today's women have new measurements: 42-56-33. Forty-two per cent of the American work force are women, Fifty-Six per cent of adult women hold paid jobs and thirty-three million are in clerical service, sales, or factory jobs, underpaid, undervalued, and under appreciated."[8] With numbers such as these, and their recent surge in activism, women workers in the United States cannot be ignored, and if recent efforts are only partially successfully, they will not allow themselves to be ignored.

Women in Business Today

Business Accepts the New Women, While the Myths Linger

Harold H. Frank wrote in 1977, "It took a decade of federal legislation, relentless agitation from the women's movement, and seismic shifts in public opinion, but women at last are moving boldly into the mainstream of corporate management. The battle for equality in blue-collar and clerical jobs moved faster because bias was easier to prove. The far more complex struggle for equal status up the corporate ladder has taken longer and is far from over. But the big news is that women are making headway, slowly in the executive suite, faster at the lower rungs of middle management."[9] According to my research, the above statement is representative of the position of the working women today, however it does appear somewhat rosier than the actuality.

During the period from 1970 to 1975, while some areas of industry still remained highly male dominated, there were changes occurring. Where changes did occur, "the percentage changes in the employment of women were almost always more favourable than the changes in the total employment in the industry. That is, if change figures were positive, then the growth rate for women was larger than the growth rate for total employment in the industry; and if the figures were negative, then the women's percentage change figure was smaller."[10]

While women were entering 'the mainstream of corporate management', for a large number of them it continued to be within the traditional areas for working women.[11]

While public opinion has changed regarding working women, their motives and desires the all too familiar concepts of 'women's, work' and other stereotypic ideas still persist. As these are in the form of deep seated attitudes and assumptions change in them will not come about quickly. Some of the myths still lingering include: women working just for 'pin money', women not wanting to work if they did not have to, and women being more satisfied than men with intellectually undemanding jobs.[12]

These myths in many cases form the basis for a self-fulfilling prophesy or Pygmalion Effect, with regard to women being considered for management. The assumptions about women, which exist in management, form their criteria for selection of potential managerial candidates. If women are assumed to be unlikely candidates for future management positions, their talents will not be nurtured, and they will not be given those assignments which will 'qualify' them when openings in management training programmes do occur. While the intent to get more women into management positions may exist, the subliminal assumptions will effectively keep women out, if they are not modified.[13]

The myths, which do exist, are greater in the ranks of the older male managers and co-workers. Younger, lower level male managers are more accepting the new role of women, although some mixed feelings also persist.[14] This can be expected from a generation which was brought up alongside many of these otherwise drastically new concepts about women, with the mixed feeling being partially induced by partially social and partially economic forces.

While women who have already made it to the executive ranks are in agreement that "sex barriers to high corporate positions and the stereotypes that go with them are rapidly fading"[15] it has not been an easy climb toward to top.

In essence, "it is all too easy, to follow the path of the past. But the past is not the present and women's aspirations have widened and their positions have changed .... Managers must ask themselves if discrimination is practised where career development is concerned and if it is practised knowingly or force of habit" [16] I concur with Alma S. through Baron, in that many managers are not aware of the old thought patterns in use and the resultant non-intentional discrimination.

Women obviously have the ability to 'make it' in business within the management ranks of the modern corporation, and management has given every indication that they want to see her there, the only area of confusion, revolves around the best way to aid her, without resorting to the traditional paternalistic approach.

As history has evidenced, legislation cannot be used in and of itself, to eliminate inequality; there is a need for it, to eliminate the legal barriers to inequality. One women who has made it, Ester Peterson, says: "My philosophy is to remove the legal barriers to equality, and that has largely been done. The doors are open, and it's up to women to move through."[17] I agree, that except for the ERA or a similar measure to remove the final legal traces of inequality, that legislation is largely in the past, in the working women's movement.

The key barriers at this point, in time and in the near future, lie in the lingering assumptions and myths, which exist in business, as they exist in society as a whole concerning the 'differences' between men and women. What is needed, is retraining and re-education, which will allow acceptance of the modern women by men, and allow the women to feel more at home acting in those traditionally male dominated situations. It is only through such retraining and re-education, that the true woman will be allowed to emerge from the constraints of society. As Dorothy Simon said, "You can't legislate acceptance."[18]

In this area, the most important teaching will not be business school type teaching, but programmes such as one used by the Prudential Insurance Company, designed to "help women develop their talents".[19]

In any such programme, the thrust of the women's training area is in assertiveness. This training is geared toward effecting "changes in both their behaviour and attitudes ... the theory underlying assertiveness training is that the submissive unassertive behaviour patterns associated with the traditional supportive status of women are largely learned, and can therefore be unlearned with the proper training and reinforcement. If women are to assume equal status with men in society, it is imperative that the habit of submission to men be broken."[20]

In any programme which is geared toward making women more willing to take their proper place in the business community, it is imperative that male managers be given assurances as to what is going on, and are allowed to participate in training aimed at shaking some of the prevalent myths about women.

While education coupled with the already rapid influx of women into top positions, it must be remembered that this approach will only give short term results, while the long term will in time begin to show actual changes in the attitudes of society toward women. It will be very long before the sweeping attitude changes can be expected.

REFERENCES

1. Margaret Cussler, *The Women Executive* (New York, New York: Harcourt, Brace and Company, 1958), p. 154.
2. *Ibid.*, p. 158.
3. *Ibid.*, p. 158.
4. Frances Maule, *Executive Careers for Women* (New York: Harper and Brothers, 1961), pp. 227-33.
5. Stimpson, ed., *Discrimination Against Women*, pp. 537-51.
6. *U.S. News and World Report (Labour)*, July 30, 1979, p. 58.
7. *Ibid.*, p. 58.
8. *Ibid.*, pp. 58-59.
9. *Ibid.*
10. Ruth Gilbert Shaeffer and Helen Axel, *Improving Job Opportunities for Women* (New York: The Conference Board, 1978), p. 32

11. Frank, *Women in the Organization,* p. 272.
12. Luthans and Hodgetts, *Social Issues in Business,* pp. 124-25.
13. Frank, *Women in the Organization,* p. 271.
14. *Ibid.,* p. 272.
15. Roger Morris, "Women at the top, "*Training and Development Journal* (May 1977), p. 39.
16. Alma S. Baron, "New data on women managers," *Training and Development Journal* (November 1978), p. 13.
17. Morris, *Women at the Top,* p. 40.
18. *Ibid.,* p. 42.
19. Barbara A. Philla, "Women in business," *Training and Development Journal* (November 1977), pp. 22-25.
20. Frank, *Women in the Organization,* p. 271.

BIBLIOGRAPHY

Abbott, Edith, *Women in Industry,* New York: Appleton and Company, 1909.

Baer, Judith, A., *The Chains of Protection,* Westport, Conneticut: Greenwood Press, 1978.

Baker, Elizabeth Faulkner, *Technology and Women's Work,* New York: Columbia University Press, 1964.

Baron, Alma, S., "New data on women managers," *Training and Development Journal,* November 1978.

Crittenden, Ann. "Study finds women lagging in craft jobs," *New York Times,* February 26, 1979.

Crittenden Ann. "Women cite neglect in United States job training," *New York Times,* February 12, 1979.

Cussler, Margaret, *The Woman Executive,* New York: Harcourt, Brace and Company, 1958.

Frank, Harold H., *Women in the Organization,* Philadelphia: University of Pennsylvania Press, 1977.

Luthans, Fred and Hodgetts, Richard M., *Social Issues in Business,* New York: Macmillan Publishing Incorporated, 1976.

Lyle, Jerolyn R and Ross, Jane L., *Women in Industry,* Lexington, Massachusetts: Lexington Books, 1973.

Maule, Frances, *Executive Careers for Women,* New York: Harper and Brothers, 1961.

Mittenthal, Sue, "After baby, whether the career," *New York Times,* February 14, 1979.

Morris, Roger, "Women at the top," *Training and Development Journal,* November 1978.

Philla, Barbara A., "Women in business," *Training and Development Journal*, November 1977.

Roberts, Steven V., "Blacks and women clash on access to jobs and aid," *New York Times*, February 20, 1979.

Shabecoff, Philip, "Jobs for December and unemployment show little change," *New York Times*, February 12, 1979.

Shaeffer, Ruth Gilbert and Axel, Helen, *Improving Job Opportunities for Women*, *New York*; The Conference Board, 1978.

Silver, Roy R., "Job help for women," *New York Times*, February 11, 1979.

Stimpson, Dr. Catherine R., *Discrimination Against Women*, New York: R.R. Bowker Co., 1973.

6

Women in the Corporate World, 2001

The women's liberation movement in India, although it started much later than in the western world, has been in existence for quite some time now. As far back as 1957, Jawaharlal Nehru said, "We talk of revolution, political and economic, and yet the greatest revolution in the country is one that affects the status and living conditions of its women."

In the last three decades there has been a remarkable change in the attitude of Indian women towards education and employment. Along with every other sphere of society, Indian corporate organizations too have felt the impact of this movement. Some changes have already taken place and others will continue to occur in the way *i.e.,* society in general, and the corporate sector in particular, view their working women members. It is the objective of this paper to analyze some of these changes and make a projection about the position of women in the organizations of the 21st century.

Historical Attitudes to Women

We cannot make any study of working women in isolation from the society we live in. "It is important to note here that while many of the problems faced by working women are universal, there are some that are unique to India. What is even more important is that the solutions to these problems may not be universal. Since the problems of Indian working women often have their roots in our social and cultural traditions, research must view the problems of Indian women within the specific socio-cultural context of Indian Society" (Ahmad, 1986).[1]

The problems that present day working women face can be traced back through history to the neolithic times when a division of labour already existed on the basis of sex and where me. hunted while women gathered roots and fruits. The earth's and women's capacity to give birth—a capacity that men lack—quite naturally gave women a prominent place in the early agricultural society (Fromm, 1973a).[2] So, at this time women and men were already doing different kinds of work, but women were not apparently subordinates to men.

This set-up, however, appears to have changed in the third millennium, when agricultural techniques advanced enough to enable large groups of people to live together and claim ownership over extensive tracts of land. At this point, many specialized jobs came into being, like producing food, building cities, etc. What is more important is that "it was discovered that man could be used as an economic instrument, that he could be exploited, that he could be made a slave" (Fromm, 1973 b).[3] With this change in attitude leading from a co-operative, mutually beneficial society to an authoritarian, centrally ruled society, the position of women also changed to one of subordination. Since that time, positions of power and authority came to be concentrated in the hands of men. This is true even in the matriarchal societies, where either property rights or managerial rights have always been held by men.

Myths of Women's Weaknesses

The question that comes to mind after so many years of the women's liberation movement is, why are there still so few of them in positions of power and responsibility? The easy answer to this question is that they lack the drive for power and for recognition. This hypothesis, however, cannot be maintained when we look at the number of women who start off on the path to build a career. A large percentage of these women have to drop out later owing to various reasons, such as that the husbands do not permit, society disapproves, the pressure of work both at home and in the office becomes too much.

All the above reasons are external to the woman herself and it is a matter of debate whether any properties like self-assertiveness or aggression are lacking in women who are thus handicapped in the struggle to reach preferred positions in society. There is probably a more complex relationship between maleness and self-assertive aggressiveness. This is no surprise to the geneticist who knows that a genetic disposition can be translated into a certain type of behaviour, but can be understood only in terms of its interconnection with other genetic dispositions and with the total life situation into which a person is born and has to live (Fromm, 1973c).[4] The fact that, inspite of such information being available to the general public, the conditions of working women still remain the same is due to the propagation of unexamined myths, accepted by both men and women.

One of these myths is that men are adept at certain jobs, while women are adept at others. While this may be partly true, there has certainly never been any scientific study conducted to find out which kinds of jobs are suited to which sex. There is however, a definite bias in the recruitment policies of organizations while selecting management personnel, though some organizations do not actively demonstrate such prejudices. An in-depth study by Sutton and Moore (1985)[5] strongly suggested that most of the problems lay in the fact that women get stereotyped into certain roles and this is enough to keep them from joining certain areas in organizations. Thus, in India, few women have been successful in areas still regarded as male preserves. For example, one lady who holds a very senior position in a large business group was once told during her interview with a multinational company in India, that she should never expect to rise to a position higher than that of a Product Manager.

In the open job market, women either hold positions of school teachers, nurses, secretaries, etc., or they are in the lower ranges of prestigious occupations like those in the administrative or managerial sector (Ahmad, 1979).[6] Even when women are as qualified as men, they tend to earn less (Jaswal, 1979).[7] These findings clearly reflect the fact that the division of the job market on the basis of sex is heavily tilted in men's favour. Even when women do succeed in certain areas which are traditionally male dominated, they often do not get credit for their competence. While male success tends to be attributed to stable personal attributes (*e.g.,* ability), female success tends to be attributed to unstable causes, such as effort or luck.

These sex based attributional patterns may be due to differential assumptions concerning the capacities of males and females. That is, if males are expected to be competent, their successes are consistent with expectations and are therefore attributed to something stable in them. In contrast, if a women is expected to do poorly in a traditionally masculine task, her success is attributed to a temporary cause such as unusual effort, so that one can continue to maintain a low expectation about her future promise. Further, reward allocation coupled with attributional biases explain why women receive fewer important rewards for equal performance. Thus the slow progress women seem to be making to the upper levels in most fields may be due in part to subtle cognitive processes.

Stereotypes of Women

Research has shown a correlation between sex rate stereotyping and people's reactions to men and women in organizational settings. The stereotyped concepts of 'women' and 'manager' were seen as incompatible, whereas 'man' and 'manager' were found to be compatible. Thus, stereotypes operate in subtle ways to limit equal employment opportunities for women.

Another myth that is firmly entrenched in Indian society is that the working women has somehow lost some of her 'goodness'. People often, consciously or sub-consciously, believe that women in positions of power have got there through bribing men with their sexuality rather than through their own capabilities. This may stem from the time when women were actually not trained for any particular job and they did have to resort to such means—

as for instance, the women who held power in the court of a king. This view has often led to the sexual harassment of working women, who are perceived to have lower moral values than non-working women. Female sexual harassment commonly follows the traditional inequitous male-female power balance. Male superior harassing female subordinate involves intimidation, since he has the power to retaliate if she resists. Male dominated occupations allow males more power than females through both occupational position and cultural stereotypes. In traditionally male occupations, male co-workers also derive power from male group support. Small number of women in traditionally male occupations will thus risk sexual harassment from both male superiors and male co-workers.

Traditional sex role socialization patterns militate against equally expressive displays of power and affiliation within mixed sex working groups. Cultural norms prescribe expression of aggressive feelings by men, while women have been taught to repress aggressive displays. Repressed anger turns to affective displays of hurt, disappointment, fear and self-recrimination. This often results in changing jobs, which, in turn, reduce the likelihood of promotion and further training based on job experience. Moreover, the women's self-image and self-confidence are damaged and her motivation to work is reduced. Finally, group responses (in most cases the group perceives the victim as having done something to deserve the harassment) to the victims of sexual harassment create a hostile work environment for women and increase the likelihood of further harassment.

Another reason why men may consider it degrading for women to work is that today the majority of women who work are actually forced to do so through depressed economic circumstances and they mainly join lowstatus and low-paid jobs (Wadhera, 1975).[8] So, in the eyes of society, these women are working because their husbands are not good enough workers to support the family.

A reason why men, find it difficult to relate to women they have to work with is that, in many cases, the social set-up is such that the only women they have interacted with earlier are those in their family. The typical image of a woman is that of a nurturing or vengeful mother. The other women likely to figure prominently at any stage are school teachers, nurses and wives who are likely to contribute to this image. Since the image that men hold in their heads and the reality faced at work are so different, men often become confused and resentful, as they would when faced with an alien phenomenon.

Role Conflicts in Women

A common observation made about women and particularly about professional women, is that they face acute role conflicts while trying to combine the two roles of working women and housewife (Ahmad, 1979).[9] Professional women mostly take up work because they want to do so and not for any other reason (Wadhera, 1975).[10] Hence, they are likely to be more serious about their work. These women at the same time have a strong commitment at home as housewife and mother, and to meet both these demands seriously becomes very difficult.

This situation is further aggravated by the fact that the two roles are so contradictory. On the one hand, women are supposed to be assertive, confident, independent, efficient and successful at work, while, on the other hand, they are expected to be non-assertive, submissive, dependent, yet very efficient in the traditional role of wife and daughter-in-law. An unco-operative husband does nothing to improve the situation.

For some time now, a few women have been aware of these problems and have tried to change the situation. Two basic problems they have had to face are the fact that: (1) Indian society is very culture and tradition conscious and, hence, resistant to change; and (2) women are now trying to gain equality in a man's world on new terms. An example of the latter point is easily found in the corporate world. Women who have made it to the top sometimes have to pay a price for their success. Consciously or sub-consciously they start acting like men, because they feel that to be like a man is the way to succeed. These women are very conscious of their own status and treat all other women in the organization as threats to their status. Once women have succeeded, they have the same prejudice against women that men do, though possibly to a lesser degree. This problem is strengthened by the attitude of recruiters who feel that masculine values and traits are more desirable in new employees than feminine characteristics.

Two studies conducted by C.D. Sutton and K.K. Moore in 1965 and 1985 showed that the percentage of women who would feel comfortable working under women managers fell from 63 per cent to 54 per cent (Sutton and Moore, 1985).[11] This could be interpreted as a reaction by the women already established in corporations to the threat of a large number of other women joining the corporate sector. So they allow only women like themselves to advance in their organization. This is basically resentment against other women who retain the femininity that they have had to sacrifice. This phenomenon has been described as the *Queen Bee Syndrome* by Taruis Gaines and Jayaratne (Jayaratne, 1974).[12]

All this suggests that in the future, the women in an organization may form an elite and discriminate against other women in the same way that men have been doing so far. This is a real possibility which may happen, unless career-oriented women carefully examine their goals and values to distinguish between what is important to them and what is a reaction against male domination.

Automation and Women

Other forces will also play a large future role in the position of women. Automation, both at home and in the work environment, is one such factor. One effect that automation has produced on the traditional housewife is that she does not have to sit in the kitchen or wash clothes all day long. She can come into contact with the outside world more often, has more time to educate herself and, in general, is more mobile then before. More and more women in the future will be freed from the drudgery of being a housewife and turn to work amongst other things.

The other influence of automation on the home is an erosion of the role of the traditional housewife. In earlier times, when a housewife cooked a meal, a whole lot of effort and care went into it. Through this effort the housewife was perceived to express her concern for the entire family. All the softer emotions in the family were projected on to the housewife, who held these feelings for the entire family. Now, however, as all domestic work gets more and more automated, the personal touch of the housewife is reduced. So, society's perception of the housewife is changing to a view that will not tie her down to the kitchen quite so much; she can be more mobile without arousing the ire of society.

In the working environment, automation will mean that there is less emphasis on manual jobs. Hence, in areas like production, one of the main bases of discrimination against women (their lack of physical strength) will no longer be valid. Automation depersonalizes work. It does not involve human interaction and it hardly matters whether it is a man or a women who presses the button to operate a machine.

As it becomes more onerous for one person to support a family, more women will take up work. Women who come from higher status families may not be satisfied with low-paid, low-status jobs. These women will take up professional careers, if they are given the freedom to work. Till now, the prestige of women has been linked to the occupational prestige of the men of the house. Usually, it is on par or one step lower (D'Souza, 1980).[13] It will be a great step forward for women, if they can de-link the two. Again, the number of women getting higher education has grown so much that it now far exceeds the number of women joining work. One way out is for women to get professional training and go in for self-employment.

Other Factors

There are some other factors in today's society that will play a part in helping women in their quest for a better working life. The practice of family planning is becoming more popular all over Asia (Ming, 1984).[14] Obviously women, not burdened with children, will find the pursuit of careers are also becoming more common, so that women will be considerably relieved in their traditional role of mother.

Women are also marrying at a later age. This will give them more time to settle down in a career and become economically independent. Such women would be free to marry on their own terms and out of personal choice, rather than for the traditional reason of ensuring bed, board and care (Ming, 1984).[15] The negative aspect of this is that the men and women of this class have not been able to work out a new family set-up where both the man and the woman work and share in domestic chores. This is one of the reasons for the increase in the number of broken marriages.

Conclusion

One thing becomes clear from an examination of these trends: the social prejudices that prevent women from leading a full and useful life are not standing up to the pressures of the fast-changing socio-economic situation. A striking example of this can be seen in Iran. Despite the attitude to women there which is due to the revival of Islamic fundamentalism, women have gone out to fight in the Gulf war.

Clearly, women will face both adverse and favourable forces in their quest for equal rights in the corporate world. The going will be tough, for however much attitudes and values may change, men will dominate for sometime to come by virtue of their sheer strength of numbers. This is why for complete equality to come about, one more assumption will have to be examined that of the "masculinity" of the male which forces him to go out and work (Jongeward and Scott, 1976).[16]

There is nothing in the research of psychologists up to the present day to indicate that man is more suited to cope with the pressures of a working life than women. On the contrary, research findings in the US indicate that in trying to cope with these pressures, men have a shorter life span than women. If one re-examining this assumption, men can dispense with the traditional ideas of their role in society, then, perhaps, the number of men competing for jobs in a progressively more competitive job market will go down and women and men will come closer to competing as human beings rather than on the basis of sex.

REFERENCES

1. Ahmad, Karuna, The Trishankus: Women in Professions in India, *Sociological Bulletin*, Vol. 33, Nos. 1 & 2, 1986.
2. Fromm, Erich, *The Anatomy of Human Destructiveness*, London, Jonathan Cape, 1973 a, pp. 213-14.
3. Fromm, Erich, *op. cit.*, p. 223.
4. Fromm, Erich, *op. cit.*, p. 262-63.
5. Sutton, CD. and Moore, K.K., Executive Women--20 Years Later, *Harvard Business Review*, September October, 1985.
6. Ahmad, Karuna, Studies of Educated Working Women in India, Trends and Issues, *Economic and Political Weekly*, Vol. 14, No. 33, 1979.
7. Jaswal, *Women in Selected Professions: A Trend Analysis of Women in Science, Engineering and Technology*, unpublished M. Phil dissertation, Zakir Hussain Centre for Educational Studies, School of Social Science, Jawaharlal Nehru University, New Delhi, 1979.
8. Wadhera, K., *New Bread Winners, New Delhi*, Vishwa Yuvak Kendra, 1975.
9. Ahmad, Karuna, *Women, Attitudes and Work*, (mimeographed), 1978.
10. Wadhera, K., *op. cit.*
11. Sutton & Moore, *op. cit.*
12. Jayaratne, J.A., Graham Staines, Carlo Taruis; The Queen Bee Syndrome. *Psychology Today*, January, 1974.
13. D'Souza, V.S., *Women in Contemporary India and South Asia*, New Delhi, Manohar Publications, 1980, p. 125.
14. Ming, To Yiu, Indicators of Development and Development of Indicators: The Case of Women's Development in Hong Kong, *Asian Exchange*, Vol. 3, No. 1, 1984.
14. Ming, *op. cit.*
16. Jongeward, D. and Dru, Scott, *Women as Winners*, Manila, Addison-Wesley, 1976.

7

Women and the Socialist System

From the very beginning, women have played an important role in trade union life and in the work of the trade unions. They are working in trade union bodies at all levels, and their active contribution is felt in all trade union activity.

The growing rate of employment of women has also been accompanied by a gradual increase in the number of women organized in trade unions. Whereas in 1955 women accounted for 33.6 per cent of all members of the Revolutionary Trade Union Movement, this figure increased to 40.6 per cent in 1963 and to 44.8 per cent at present.

The number of women holding trade union functions is also rising every year. In 1955, women were 26.9 per cent of the total number of trade union officials in the Revolutionary Trade Union Movement's branch organizations. This figure increased in 1963 to 31.1 per cent and to as much as 41.4 per cent at present. A similar trend in the representation of women can be seen in the Central Council of Trade Unions. Whereas in 1946 women were 10.4 per cent of all the members of this supreme trade union body, this figure increased to 22.7 per cent in 1955, to 26 per cent in 1963 and to 37.1 per cent at present.

Of late, women have been represented in leading trade union functions as follows:

Function	*Number of women*
Secretary of the Central Council of Trade Unions	1
Secretary of the Czech Trade Union Council	1
Chairmen of Central Committees of Trade Unions (18 Unions)	7
Deputy Chairmen of Central Committees of Trade Unions	7
Chairmen of Czech Trade Unions Committees	3
Chairman of Slovak Trade Unions Committees	4
Deputy Chairmen of Czech Trade Unions Committees	1
Deputy Chairmen of Slovak Trade Unions Committees	3
Chairmen of Regional Trade Unions Committees	26
Chairmen of District Trade Unions Councils	2

I

Although the percentage of women holding leading functions greatly increased after the 8th All-Union Congress in 1972 compared with the preceding period, their share in the life of the trade unions must be further raised, especially by their training for higher trade union functions. Part of this training is in holding functions in lower trade union bodies where officials get the necessary experience and, in particular, their training in trade union schools and courses. The Central Council of Trade Unions and the Slovak Trade Union Council arrange many kinds of trade union schooling as well as short-term and long-term courses at their Central Schools which are attended by many women. Since 1972, these schools have also been organizing one-year extra-mural courses on trade union policy in which one class is reserved exclusively for women trade union officials. Women who are expected to be entrusted with higher trade union functions are also sent to the Central School of the Soviet Trade Unions in Moscow. Besides these higher forms of trade union study, women officials also train for their functions in the current system of trade union schooling, at seminars, gatherings of trade union activists, meetings of women, etc., which are organized at all levels. Reports on important aspects of trade union policy are delivered at these events by leading trade union officials, including Secretaries of the Central Council of Trade Unions.

The Revolutionary Trade Union Movement consequently endeavours to raise the number of women taking part in trade union work and their qualifications for this work. In this way, it fulfils also one of its basic functions—to train potential cadres for other leading bodies in the national economy and in the administration of the State. Many women who have gained experience, practical knowledge and sound self-confidence in many-sided trade union activities, have later taken up leading economic and other functions, and are successful as deputies in representative bodies, as officials of other social organizations, etc.

About 40 per cent of all the trade union officials helping successfully to implement the demanding tasks of the Revolutionary Trade Union Movement are women. This proves that its attention has especially in recent years been concentrating not only on the creation of favourable conditions for the life and work of women but also on ensuring their ever greater and more active share in trade union functions, because they acquit themselves well, introduce new elements into trade union work, display initiative, are consistent and also critical. They are not content with a superficial approach to problems, and formalism, and are successful in persuading other women-workers to fulfil the production targets at work and the programmatic aims of the trade union organization.

The orientation and further expansion of women's share in trade union functions, which was emphasized by the Revolutionary Trade Union Movement in a number of documents and resolutions adopted already before its 8th Congress, proved to be correct and beneficial. The larger number of women holding trade union functions is also reflected in the undeniable successes the Czechoslovak trade unions have been attaining recently.

An important role in trade union work among women and in the implementation of the ambitions tasks of the Revolutionary Trade Union Movement is played by women's commissions which are auxiliary bodies of the trade union shop and works committees and of higher trade union bodies.

In fulfilling their tasks, the women's commissions co-operate with the other commissions in enterprises as well as higher trade union bodies and take the initiative in submitting proposals for the solution of problems affecting the life and work of women to the bodies which established them. They engage in effective organizational and educational activities, win over women for active participation in the realization of trade union policy, and participate in creating conditions so that women may raise their ideological, political and professional level. They help to increase women's participation in the solution of economic tasks, in improving the working environment and working conditions, and in meeting the legitimate claims and interests of working women.

The women's commissions attain good result in the field of working conditions and working environment *e.g.* by seeing that measures designed to rationalize production lead to better conditions for women, that the inventors' and innovators' movement be used for easing work where mainly women are employed, etc. They insist on the work and working environment being in harmony with the principles of socialist culture of work. They concentrate on creating suitable social conditions for women, *e.g.* in raising qualifications and making full use of them, on correct remuneration for work, on care for the children of workers, on appropriate adjustment of working hours for women who have small children, on improvement of health care, on provision of services easing housework and saving women's time, etc.

Women's commissions and other women officials of the trade unions can be credited with the establishment at enterprises of women's rest corners, with the introduction of refrigerators and buffets selling beverages at places of work, with the installation of adequate airconditioning, with the provision of cloak-rooms and showers, as well as hairdresser and pedicure centres, the provision of electric massage equipment for women, etc. Women's commissions in many cases have also been responsible for the building of creches or nursery schools and for the introduction of such services as the despatch of clothes for dry-cleaning and linen to laundries.

Women's commissions often intervene on behalf of women living alone who are family breadwinners. They help to get priority acceptance into pre-school institutions and young pioneer camps for their children and for children of large families. Women's commissions help in other fields as well. For example, they have taken over the rearing of children who have lost both parents, in other cases they have helped to provide a flat for a single mother, etc.

The women's commissions also concentrate on more demanding tasks, especially in the field of organizational work among women and of their political education. They persuade women to play a greater part in the development of initiative at work, in the inventors' and innovators' movement, in brigades promoting comprehensive rationalization, in assistance to women workers who, for various reasons, are lagging behind in the fulfilment of their tasks at work, etc.

Women's commissions also stimulate the ambition of women to excel in their profession, they use technical and economic propaganda to acquaint women with new methods and procedures at work, they help to create pre-requisites and conditions for women constantly to raise their qualifications so that they may be well prepared for making an active contribution to the solution of the tasks ensuing from the rapidly advancing technization, mechanization and automation of production.

All this shows the many-sided character of the activities of women's commissions where the women assert their natural talents and help solve the present as well as long-term needs and interests of women. Together with other women officials of the trade unions, they also encourage women to take a greater and more committed part in the development of trade union work.

The Czechoslovak Union of Women

The Czechoslovak Union of Women is the central organization of Czechoslovak women. Through its activities in the field of political education it is winning over women for participation in public life and is also training them in its organizations to become future officials of other organizations of the National Front.

The main tasks of the Czechoslovak Union of Women are focussed on educating people for socialism and instilling in them a correct understanding of the mission of women in the socialist society.

The Czechoslovak Union of women plays an important role in the shaping and strengthening of the socialist family, especially in efforts to make purposive use of and to expand the conditions created by the Czechoslovak society for harmonizing a woman's mission at work, as a mother and as a citizen.

The Czechoslovak Union of Women participates in the management and administration of the State, takes the initiative in submitting proposals for the solution of questions concerning the position of women under socialism, helps to train women for active participation in public life and proposes the best of them for election to representative bodies and to other functions.

The Union of Women co-operates with State bodies, National Committees, the National Front (which associates all political and social organizations), the Revolutionary Trade Union Movement and other social organizations and scientific institutions in providing the best possible conditions for the all-round development of woman's personality.

The latest Congress of the Czechoslovak Union of Women, held in April 1974, emphasized that the Union will endeavour to play a greater part in strengthening the moral and political unity of all the Czechoslovak people, in the development of mass-based political and educational work among women, in the creation of a socialist atmosphere at work and in life. It emphasized that the Czechoslovak Union of Women is an important social organization, a movement with pronounced political objectives and important tasks in the realization of the ambitious ideals of the socialist society.

An important task facing the Czechoslovak Union of Women is to promote development of international co-operation of the progressive women of the whole world in the struggle for the preservation of peace, for social progress, for a better life for women all over the world. As a member of the International

Democratic Women's Federation, the Union can maintain broad contacts with woman's organizations of all continents. Czechoslovak women are linked by the firmest ties of deep and unshakable friendship with Soviet women form whom they drew strength and experience already in the days of the pre-Munich Republic in their struggle against capitalism and all forms of oppression. Today, they are learning from Soviet women how to make a more universal, better and more effective contribution to the development of the socialist society which women are actively influencing and which, in turn, continuously shapes their personality and their further development.

The Czechoslovak Union of Women maintains traditional relations of sisterly co-operation with women in other socialist countries, with whom it makes a broad exchange of experience gained in all spheres of the life of the society. A deep knowledge of the work and life of women in socialist countries is of great help to Czechoslovak women.

The Czechoslovak Union of Women is also promoting good relations with progressive women's organizations in many capitalist and developing countries and is inviting delegations from these countries to the Czechoslovak Socialist Republic so that they may see for themselves the positions held by women in the Czechoslovak society, their rights and gains. It also organizes campaigns of solidarity with the women's movement in various parts of the world, in which Czechoslovak women take a very active part on a mass scale.

The different bodies of the Czechoslovak Union of Women have special commissions which gather comments and suggestions submitted by women from all fields and ideal with them.

These include *e.g.*, commissions for political education which concentrate mainly on political and cultural work among women. They arrange meetings of women to discuss important aspects of the various spheres of the life of the society, give lectures, hold debates, seminars, etc. The commissions for employed women give their attention to places where the majority of workers are women and check whether the legal regulations issued in the interest of women are consistently observed.

The agricultural commissions help to raise the cultural level of women's life and work in the villages and to improve their qualifications. Fro example, the commissions organize excursions to particularly successful Unified Agricultural Co-operatives to promote exchange of experience, arrange discussion evenings and meetings of women doing different jobs in agriculture and are a great help in improving the range of products supplied to village shops.

The main task of commissions for the family and education is to train young people for parenthood. In co-operation with the Socialist Union of Youth these commissions arrange lectures on child-care, on fostering the child's emotions, etc. The speakers at these meetings are women doctors, psychologists and pedagogical workers whose services are engaged by the Czechoslovak Union of Women. Particularly creditable work is done by these commissions in the districts for which they are responsible in attention to broken marriages and to the children of them.

Important tasks are being also fulfilled by the commissions for shops and services. They discuss with the producers, trading enterprises and enterprises providing services the complaints, comments and suggestions of women, gathered at various meetings, discussion evenings and from letters. The commissions then negotiate measures to redress shortcomings with the respective officials. Another task facing these commissions is the creation of a network of shops convenient both for women who are consumers and women working in them.

The Czechoslovak Union of Women has almost 600,000 members and their number is constantly rising.

Czechoslovak Women in the Struggle for Peace and International Solidarity of the Working People

Together with other Czechoslovak working people, Czechoslovak women are members of the largest international trade union centre, the World Federation of Trade Unions (WFTU) which, strictly adhering to class principles, proletarian internationalism and international working class solidarity, has for 30 years been waging a relentless struggle for a better life of the working people, for social progress, national independence, democracy and peace.

The World Federation of Trade Unions, which is fully aware of the part played by women at work and in the life of the society, as well as of the size of the militant potential in their ranks, has given extraordinary attention since its establishment in 1945 to problems of working women. It convened three world trade union conferences of working women to discuss their main problems and map out further action: in 1958 in Budapest, in 1984 in Bucharest, and the third, in April 1972, in Prague. Czechoslovak women trade unionists fully participated in organizing this conferences and in ensuring its successful course.

Czechoslovak women also fully endorsed the Charter of economic, social, cultural and trade union rights of working women, which was unanimously passed by this Conference and the demands of which have already been practically realized in socialist Czechoslovakia.

The ideas and the conclusions of the 3rd World Trade Union Conference on the problems of working women were also reflected in the proceedings of the 8th All-Union Congress held in Prague in June 1972 which also elaborated in its resolution the programme mapped out by the 14th Congress of the Communist Party of Czechoslovakia for the further comprehensive expansion of care for working women.

Since the creation of the WFTU, Czechoslovak women trade unionists have actively participated in the work of the World Federation of Trade Unions and of its Trade Union Internationals (TUI). They also hold important functions in the leading bodies of the Trade Union Internationals; the working group of the World Federation of Trade Unions for questions concerning working women is also headed by a Czechoslovak woman trade unionist, a Secretary of the Central Council of the Czechoslovak Trade Unions.

Czechoslovak women are promoting traditional and long-standing co-operation with the women of the socialist countries, especially of the Soviet Union, from whom they learn progressive methods of work applied in the most various sectors of economic life, and with whom they exchange experience. The sisterly ties existing between the women of Czechoslovak Socialist Republic and of the Soviet Union were forged in joint struggles against the fascist enemy, as well as in the construction of socialism. Czechoslovak women fully realize that without the fraternal assistance of the Soviet Union there would be no free Czechoslovakia and the Czechoslovak people could build socialism in their country.

The women of the Czechoslovak Socialist Republic are also linked by firm ties of solidarity with the progressive women of many capitalist and developing countries and their militant organizations.

Czechoslovak women have played their part in the international policy of the Czechoslovak State and in campaigns expressing and supporting international solidarity. Campaigns of solidarity with the heroic people of Vietnam, with the struggle of the Chilean patriots against the fascist military junta, with the Arab people fighting against Israeli aggressions and for the victory of their legitimate cause, with the fight of the nations against imperialism, for freedom and independence, have become in our country large nation-wide movements to which an important contribution was made by working women.

Czechoslovak women proclaimed many years ago a clear motto which retains its validity: "Build up your country and you strengthen peace." The implementation of this motto at all places of work continues to be one of the main aims of all our women.

Czechoslovak women attach extraordinary importance to the initiative taken by the United Nations by proclamation of the International Women's Year—1975. They realize that the campaigns and events organized in this year may not only greatly help towards meeting the basic requirements and interests of women all over the socialist world.

In the Marxist perspective, the abolition of private property and its replacement by social ownership and control of the means of production were viewed as the fundamental preconditions for the emancipation of women. Two structural changes were considered crucial to effect a radical change in the status of women *viz.*: *(a)* reintroduction of women into social production, and *(b)* socialization of domestic work and the care of children.

II

Advance of Women

After the revolution in the U.S.S.R. and the East European countries private property rights in the means of production were gradually eliminated and the state socialist sector attained a decisive weight in the secondary and territory spheres. In agriculture, most of the land was brought under the collective/ co-operative sector in the U.S.S.R. and Czechoslovakia while in Poland and Yugoslavia small-scale private production remained significant (Table 7.1). There was a massive and rapid increase in the number of women participating in social production. The heavy destruction of industry, power stations, housing, etc.,

Table 7.1

Some Basic Information: U.S.S.R.* : Poland, Czechoslovakia and Yugoslavia

	U.S.S.R.	*Czechoslovakia*	*Poland*	*Yugoslavia*
Population in 000 (1979)	262442	15247	35225	22160
Ownership in agriculture (1975) (% land)				
State	64.9	30.3	16.7	10.5
Co-operative	33.6	60.5	1.6	3.1
Private and other	1.5	9.2	81.3	85.1
Share of socialist sector in:				
Gross agricultural production (1975)	100.0	96.4	20.0	23.1
National income (1975)	100.0	99.5	86.1	82.4
Average monthly wages and salaries	168** ***roubles	2640 Koruna	5755 Zloty	7000 Dinars

Notes: * The term "U.S.S.R." would refer here to the present C.I.S.

** 232 roubles including allowances and benefits.

*** 1 US Dollar equals approximately 0.8 Rouble, 6 Koruna, 34 Zloty and 40 Dinars.

Sources : *(i)* Economic Survey of Europe in 1980, U.N., p. 158.

(ii) Economics of the European Socialist Countries, pp. 26-27.

during the war posed a challenging task of reconstruction and demanded mobilization of labour on a massive scale. The fact that thousands of men from the active work-force were killed during the war meant that women had to take up a variety of tasks and responsibilities in the reconstruction work. The network for schooling and training was vastly expanded and there was rapid progress in women's education.[1] (Table 7.2 to 7.5). Women

Table 7.2

Educational Attainment in the U.S.S.R.: Percentage Distribution of Women and Men by Educational

Educational Level	*Women**		*Men***	
	1939	*1969*	*1939*	*1969*
Higher Education	0.4	1.6	0.9	2.1
Secondary Education	6.7	25.5	8.8	27.3
Less than 7 years	92.9	72.9	90.3	70.6
	*Women****		*Total****	
	1969	*1980*	*1969*	*1980*
Higher Education	3.4	6.1	4.2	7.2
Secondary Education	22.7	40.7	25.6	44.4
Less than 7 years	73.9	53.2	70.3	48.4

Notes: * 16-54 years of age; ** 16-59 year of age.
*** For Population 20 years and above.

Sources : *(i)* Dodge, pp. 144-45.
(ii) Economics Role of Women, p. 87.

Table 7.3

Percentage Distribution of Population Aged 25 Years and above by Level of Education

Educational Level	*Czechoslovakia*				*Poland*		*Yugoslavia*	
	Women		*All*		*1980*		*1981*	
	1961	*1980*	*1961*	*1980*	*Women*	*All*	*Women*	*All*
Post-secondary	0.9	2.1	2.4	4.1	4.2	5.4	2.1	3.9
Secondary	12.1	25.6	13.7	38.2	17.0	20.7	8.8	15.3
Primary or less	86.9	72.3	83.9	57.8	78.8	73.9	89.2	80.8

Source : Economic Role of Women, pp. 86-87.

Table 7.4

Progress of Education in Poland: Percentage Distribution of Employed Women and Men by Educational Level

Educational Level	Women		Men	
	1968	1983	1968	1983
University graduate	3.2	5.3	4.0	6.2
Secondary vocational	10.8	20.1	5.0	12.0
General secondary	6.5	8.9	3.3	2.9
Primary vocational	4.7	14.6	9.9	22.2
Primary	42.8	38.8	39.8	44.1
No schooling	32.0	12.3	38.0	12.6

Source : The working women in Peoples Poland, p. 8.

Table 7.5

Education in Yugoslavia: Percentage Distribution of Women and Total Population (10+years) by Educational Level

Educational Level	Women		All	
	1963	1981	1963	1981
High School and above	0.3	1.7	0.6	2.8
Secondary School	3.8	10.0	6.6	15.2
4—7 grades Primary School	43.7	56.1	50.1	57.4
1—3 grades Primary School	16.4	10.0	17.3	9.5
No Schooling	35.8	22.2	25.4	15.1

Source : Women in Yugoslavia, pp. 9-10.

accepted several challenging and new vocations traditionally considered as "men's work", in addition to the feminine vocations. (Tables 7.6 to 7.13). Work outside home was now to be the focus of women's life (as men's) and women entered social production with enthusiasm and passion. This change had profound implications in terms of women's confidence, their concern with intellectual and social problems and their involvement in public affairs.

Domestic Work

In relation to the other essential task, socialization of domestic work and child care, the progress was necessarily slow. There was the question of priorities in reconstruction work. Machines, factories, railroads and power stations had to come first; housing, nurseries cafeterias and the like had to wait. Moreover, when the previously unpaid domestic work became a wage work, it tended to be expensive. The performance of social services like laundry and cooking can become effective when it is possible to replace manpower by machines to a significant extent and then alone can it be reasonably priced. The socialist economies could not take up this task on a priority basis. Moreover, a ready developed technology was not available from the West as the industry in the U.S.A. and Western Europe is interested in promoting newer and newer household appliances and gadgets and not in the mass-scale public services. In the initial years attempts were made to expand the public services, but they were labour intensive and had to be subsidized.

After the economic reforms introduced in the mid-sixties, the subsidy element in the public services got reduced.[2] In the post-reform period when a rise in income and levels of living was experienced, the expectations regarding the quality of services also underwent a change. For example, in an eating place a high standard in the quality and variety of the food served is expected yet the food must not be more expensive than the one cooked at home. The problem of providing child care facilities, particularly the care of very young children (up to 3 years), is still more complex. The location and the timings of the creche must be well adjusted to the convenience of the parents, the personnel in charge has to be adequate in number and well-trained; consequently the costs of child care tend to be quite high.[3]

In view of the difficulties of automation of the services and in the face of changing consumer preferences the path of mechanizing domestic work through home appliances got tacitly accepted during the seventies. Subsequently a considerable increase was recorded in the number of households possessing domestic appliances. (Table 7.14). This has helped ease the work; yet each woman has to spare the time individually for this work. Shopping also tends to be somewhat demanding because of the uncertainties

Table 7.6

Women in Work Force in the U.S.S.R., Czechoslovakia and Poland

		U.S.S.R.	*Czechoslovakia*	*Poland*
Female population (000)	1960	117451	6992	15260
	1980	130966	7352	16696
% in Total population	1960	54.8	51.2	51.6
	1980	53.9	51.3	51.4
Women in work force as percentage of total female population	1960	48.2	37.8	40.2
	1980	45.4	42.6	46.0
Women in work force as % in labour force	1960	51.4	41.0	43.4
	1980	50.5	44.5	45.8
Percentage distribution of working women				
Agriculture	1960	49.3	30.9	59.4
	1970	26.3	16.9	46.6
Industry	1960	22.8	35.4	16.9
	1970	31.3	40.3	32.2
Services	1960	27.9	33.7	23.7
	1970	42.4	42.8	30.2

Source : Women at Work, No. 1/1987, p. 8.

Table 7.7

Share of Women in Total Employment in the U.S.S.R.

Sector	*1930* *% women*	*1945* *% women*	*1984* *% women*
Industry	28.0	51	46
State farms	27.0	61	43
Construction	9.6	32	29
Transport	9.7	29	25
Trade	22.0	69	74
Education and Science	52.3	73	63
Total	26.7	55	49

Source : Dodge, pp. 178-79.

Table 7.8

Share of Women in Total Employment in Selected Branches in the Soviet Union and Czechoslovakia

Sector	U.S.S.R.		Czechoslovakia	
	1960 % women	1985 % women	1960 % women	1985 % women
Manufacturing and mining	45	49	38	41
Construction	30	28	12	16
Transport	24	24	17	21
Communications	64	68	51	63
Trade	66	76	68	73
Education	70	73	60	68
Science and Research	42	50	29	35
Health and Social Care	85	84	73	79
Public Administration	51	65	43	55
Banking and Insurance	68	82	54	72
All Sectors	47	51	43	45

Source : Economic Role of Women, p. 38

Table 7.9

Proportion of Women in Total Employment in Selected Branches in Poland

	1950 % women	1984 % women	1988 % women
Industry	30.3	39.3	38.5
Building	13.8	17.9	N.A.
Transport and Communications	13.3	24.1	25.2
Education, Culture and Arts	56.0	66.9	*
Health Service and Social Welfare	68.7	77.9	80.3
Finance and Social Insurance	N.A.	78.0	81.3
State Administration and Law	N.A.	56.9	58.8
Total (excluding Agriculture)	31.9	42.5	43.0

Note: * Education—73.5%; Culture and arts 60.1%.

Sources : *(i)* The Working Women in Poland, p. 7.

(ii) Facts About Poland, Ref. PF. III 8.1.

Table 7.10

Share of Employed Women in Total Employment by Type of Activity in Yugoslavia

	1954 % *women*	*1986* % *women*
Economic activities	21.5	2.5
Manufacturing, mining and quarrying	24.4	33.6
Construction	8.3	9.1
Transport and communication	11.0	13.9
Trade and catering	32.4	48.9
Non-economic activities*	41.8	57.6
Total	24.8	34.5

* Culture and social welfare and social activities and state agencies.

Source : Women in Yugoslavia, p. 14.

Table 7.11-A

Women in Selected Industries in the U.S.S.R., (1982)

Industry	% *women*
Ferrous metallurgy	29.4
Oil refining	38.1
Machine building and metal working	38.9
Chemical	50.6
Cement	36.3
Clothing	82.0
Leather and fur	62.6
Shoe	64.1
Food	54.4

Source : Dodge, pp. 180-81.

Table 7.11-B

Women Among All Specialists with Higher Education Employed in the U.S.S.R.

Speciality	*1941* % *women*	*1984* % *women*
Total	34	53
Engineers	15	31
Economists	31	63
Legal personnel	15	32
Physicians	61	74
Agronomists, foresters, Veterinarians	25	41

Source : Dodge, p. 194

Table 7.12

Share of Women in Selected Occupations in the U.S.S.R., Czechoslovakia, Poland and Yugoslavia (1980)

Occupation	*U.S.S.R. % Women*	*Czechoslovakia % Women*	*Poland % Women*	*Yugoslavia % Women*
Architects, engineers and related technicians	45.4	20.4	23.0	19.8
Medical doctors	71.7	42.2	50.9	36.6
Teachers—University and higher education	43.0	34.2	33.7	28.1
Administrative and managerial workers	20.6	14.8	27.1	8.8
Clerical and related workers	84.9	74.5	60.6	49.2
Metal processers	68.3	25.6	19.9	11.6
Chemical processers and related workers	72.0	61.9	57.7	44.8
Precision instrument makers	9.3	11.9	4.3	4.1
Blacksmiths, toolmakers, machine-tool operators	26.8	21.2	12.8	7.7

Source : Economic Role of Women, pp. 40-43.

Table 7.13

Women Specialist in Industry in Czechoslovakea (1980)

Industry	*% Women among total specialists*	*% Women with higher education among specialists with higher education*
Iron and steel	22	8
Non-ferrous metals	21	6
Rubber and chemicals	32	18
Engineering and metal processing	27	8
Wood processing	35	11
Food	45	23
Textiles	49	20
Clothing	65	16
Printing	51	20
All Industry	31	10

Source : Hietlinger, p. 152.

of supplies. Thus the working women, unlike the men, have to undertake two jobs or one may say four jobs *viz.* the paid job, domestic work, care of children and serving the husband. The men are expected to share the domestic work. The men do help in shopping or playing with the children but housework is still considered to be women's work.[4]

Progress in the Career

Women have entered the sphere of social production at a rapid rate and taken up a variety of occupations,[5] but their progress in these has been limited due to a variety of factors. Firstly, because of the heavy household responsibilities they do not find adequate time to improve their qualifications[6] and are often reluctant to accept positions of special/high responsibility. Under such a situation, *i.e.,* when they cannot work to their best ability at the job, at times, there arises a tendency to put in the best effort in the housework where traditionally they have an established superiority. If housework thus takes precedence over the paid job the progress of women in their careers gets further hampered.

The involvement of women in the social and political spheres is much less than that in the economic sphere. Even in the economic sphere, they remain within a relatively narrow range of positions. For men the career spectrum is much broader; this makes it easier for them to reach political positions which can prove useful to 'build' the career. The women also tend to be reluctant to reach up to levels where they may be required to accept positions of responsibility in the party as it is difficult to "refuse" once you go up the ladder and hence there is a tendency to remain at the middle positions. Even though the number of women participating in the socio-political bodies at various levels is not small (Table 7.15) they have yet to reach the highest bodies.[7] Such positions of authority demand almost a total commitment—a high degree of concentration and time allocation. Since women cannot yet devote themselves to their career in the same way as men can they tend to remain away from positions of authority. The fact that the number of women who have assumed very high positions is small, despite the large number of women in

Table 7.14

Possession of Household Durables in the U.S.S.R., Czechoslovakia, Poland and Yugoslavia

	Washing machine	*Refrigerator/ cooler*	*Vacuum cleaner*	*Kitchen range*	*Boiler*
U.S.S.R. (Units per 100 families)					
1960	4	4	N.A.		
1965	21	11	7		
1978	70	78	24		
Czechoslovakia (Units per 100 families)					
1953	18	2	N.A.	10	
1965	67	30	N.A.	37	
1971	91	61	N.A.	52	
Poland (1979) (Units per 100 families)					
Employee	103	94	88		
Peasant	92	59	32		
Yugoslavia: (Percentage of households possessing durables)					
All Households:					
1968	10.9	25.1	15.0	36.9	14.4
1973	34.9	53.5	29.6	60.7	28.9
Workers Households:					
1968	21.3	48.8	31.5	68.9	28.6
1973	59.7	79.8	55.3	86.7	47.6

Source : *(i)* The U.S.S.R. in figures for 1988, p. 206.

(ii) The Development of Czechoslovakia Economy, p. 193.

(iii) Poland: Statistical Data, 1981, p. 26.

(iv) Women in Yugoslavia, p. 28.

Table 7.15

Share of Women in the Representative Political Bodies and in the Communist Party in Selected Socialist Countries

U.S.S.R.	*Mid sixties % women*	*Mid seventies % women*	*Poland*	*Mid seventies % women*
Supreme Soviet of the U.S.S.R.	28.0	32	Seym	21
Supreme Soviet of Union Republics	33.7	35	People Councils	28
Supreme Soviet of Autonomous Republics	34.9	39	Residents Self-Government	30*
Territorial, regional, district, city and rural Soviets	42.8	50*		
Community Party	20	23	Polish United Workers party	23

(Contd.)

Yugoslavia	*1958 % women*	*1967 % women*	*1974 % women*
SFRY Assembly	7.0	13.3	13.6
Assemblies of Republics and Provinces	10.6	13.6	18.5
Commune Assemblies	6.0	9.4	15.2

Note: * Approximately.

** Prior to 1974 data relate to deputies with representative assembly system, for 1974 to delegates within delegation system.

Sources : *(i)* Vesnova Sarfanova p. 100; U.S.S.R. Year books.

(ii) Facts about Poland.

(iii) Women in Yugoslavia, p. 31.

employment, lends support to the age-old belief that "women are not competent to assume such positions", "they lack authority in dealing with the workers because they don't know how to rant and rave as required" or "our people love and respect women but do not obey them".

Reproduction

The near-total incorporation of women in paid employment and the increased interest in the career apparent among the women[8] was closely associated with the trend of declining birth rates in the socialist countries (Table 7.16). In response to this situation, a policy of upgrading the family's social role[9] and particularly its place in educational function got emphasized.

Table 7.16

Births, Deaths and Abortions in the U.S.S.R., Czechoslovakia, Poland and Yugoslavia

	No. of live births per 1000 population			*No. of abortions per 100 pregnancies*			*(Rate per 1000)*	
							Crude birth rate	*Crude birth rate*
	1953	*1967*	*1983*	*1953*	*1967*	*1983*	*1989*	*1989*
U.S.S.R.	25.1	17.4	15.5	—	N.A.	—	18.2*	9.7*
Czechoslovakia	21.1	15.1	18.9	10.1	36.0	22.9	17.8	11.5
Poland	29.1	16.7	17.4	17.4	30.5	25.8	19.5	9.2
Yugoslavia	28.8	18.8	15.5	—	N.A.	—	17.1	8.6

* for 1978.

Sources : *(i)* Jan Car, p. 70.

(ii) Demographic year book U.N., 1989, pp. 174-75

Co-operation between the nuclear family and public institutions was advocated. The schemes of maternity leave and maternity and child benefits were expanded (Tables 7.17, 7.18, 7.19).

Facility for unpaid maternity leave was introduced in Czechoslovakia and Poland in 1968.[10] This permits mothers to stay at home to look after their children up to 2 to 3 years of age. Employment relationship is not broken and acquired rights in respect of length of service, social security and pension

Table 7.17

Monthly Rate of Children's Allowance in Czechoslovakia

	*1948**	*1968-1972*	*1986*
		(amount in KCS)	
One child	30	90	90
2 Children	70	330	430
3 Children	120	680	880
4 Children	180	1030	1280

* Calculated in present currency.

Source: Social Guarantees in Czechoslovakia, pp. 17, 26.

Table 7.18

Monthly Family Allowance in Poland (form 1 August 1985)

	Income upto 1400 zl. per person	*Income above 1400 zl. per person*
	zl.	zl.
One chiid	160	70
Second child	250	105
Third child	340	135
Every additional child	360	155

Source : Facts About Poland, Ref. PF IV 7-1.

Table 7.19

Maternity Leave and Other Facilities in the Selected Socialist Countries

	Paid maternity leave (weeks)		*% pay protected*	*Subsequent unpaid leave*
	One child	*Twin*		
U.S.S.R.	16	18***	100	1
Czechoslovakia	26*	35	90	3
Poland	16	26****	100	3
Yugoslavia	15**		100	

Notes
* In 1966, paid maternity leave was extended from 22 weeks to 26.
** This is the minimum provided under the Federal Law. In certain Republics there are special or more liberal provisions. In Slovenia, father can take a part of the post-maternity leave in the place of mother.
*** Medical complications and/or multiple bith.
**** 26 weeks for multiple birth and 18 weeks for second child.

are preserved. This measure together with the provisions made for sizable child care grants,[11] in a way transforms maternity into paid social labour. As maternity is given this new social recognition, the traditional sexual division of labour gets re-inforced. Increases in children's allowance and other facilities are also offered. For example, in Czechoslovakia the monthly children's allowance has been raised considerably, especially for two or more children. The children's allowance for three children (880 KCS) works to about 50 per cent of the average salary of a working woman. In addition, a loan scheme was introduced in 1973, that has a provision to write off a part of the loan after the birth of a child.[12]

Public child care facilities[13] were developed rapidly in the post-revolution period[14] (Table 7.20). These services are largely financed by the state, as well as trade unions and undertakings.

Table 7.20

Day Nurseries (Creche) and Kindergarten in the U.S.S.R., Czechoslovakia and Poland

(No. of place in 000)

Year	*U.S.S.R.*		*Year*	*Czechoslovakia*		*Year*	*Poland*	
	Creche	*Kinder garten*		*Creche*	*Kinder garten*		*Creche**	*Kinder garten*
1917	2.2	N.A.	1948	6.0	205.4	1960	51.5	421.7
1928	62.0	130.0	1950	22.2	256.3	1980	64.9	607.1
1932	600.9	1061.7	1960	41.3	285.9	1986	103.6	1222.9
1940	824.1	1171.5	1965	63.3	330.1			
1957	1046.0	2095.0	1972	66.9	395.3			
1961	1574.2	3371.5	1986	74.0	522.0			
1964	2253.2	4737.3						
1988	13300							

Note: * No. of users in the respective years were 92500, 126600 and 194200.

Sources: *(i)* Dodge, pp. 28, 84; U.S.S.R., Year-Book, 1980, p. 154.

(ii) The Development of the Czechoslovakia Economy, p. 196; Statisticka rocenka CSSR, 1977, pp. 537, 579.

(iii) Poland, Statistical Data, 1981, pp. 69, 76.

At present about 10 to 15 per cent of the children (0.3 years) are looked after in creches, the facility being more widespread in the urban centres as compared to the rural areas. The young mothers, in some cases, are able to obtain help from some relatives. Otherwise the extension of maternity leave which means an interruption in the career becomes inevitable.

Status of Women

The fact that women have not yet gained equality with men in their career and remain in larger numbers at the lower and middle levels gets also reflected in the levels of earnings.[15] The earnings of women, on an average, tend to be relatively low as compared to that of men (Tables 7.21, 7.22, 7.23).

Table 7.21

Percentage Distribution of Men and Women Workers by Tariff Category in Selected Industrial Establishments in the U.S.S.R., (1980-1982)

		*Tariff Category**						
		I	*II*	*III*	*IV*	*V*	*VI*	*Average*
Machine building	M	5.8	17.2	24.6	26.6	21.1	4.7	3.5
	F	29.1	38.6	26.8	4.4	1.0	0.1	2.1
Bakeries and biscuit manufacturing	M	0.5	1.9	7.5	37.1	39.9	13.1	4.5
	F	3.9	9.7	21.1	27.8	29.3	8.2	3.9
Meat & Milk processing	M	—	4.2	27.1	31.2	34.4	3.1	4.0
	F	0.5	9.9	3.5	23.4	3.2	0.5	3.1
Textile Industry	M	14.8	11.1	12.0	17.6	18.5	26.0	3.8
	F	—	8.3	50.0	36.7	3.3	1.7	3.7

Note: * Wages are equal for men and women in each tariff category (qualificaton class); but tariff levels differ by industry, *e.g.*, average tariff category 3.9 corresponds to about 85 roubles per month in bakeries and biscuit manufacturing whereas in textile in industry average tariff category 3.7 corresponds to about 95 roubles per month.

Source: Economic Role fo Women, p. 61.

Table 7.22-A

Income Structure in the Socialist Sector in Czechoslovakia (1980)

Monthly Income (in KCS)	*% Men*	*% Women*
up to — 1400	6	40
1401 — 2000	28	46
2001 — 3000	51	13
3001 and above	15	1
Average	2336	1565

Source : Hietlinger, p. 154.

Table 7.22-B

Average Earnings in Different Occupations in Poland (1981)

	Women as % of total employed	*Average monthly wage*	*% women earning average wage or less*	*% men earning average wage or less*
Industry	39.5	2873	85.2	38.0
Construction	17.4	3471	90.2	61.3
Transport & communications	24.1	2933	89.2	49.0
Education	76.6	2566	68.7	30.2
Health	79.9	2433	63.2	36.9
Trade	72.8	2321	75.6	44.2
Total	42.3	2798	84.5	43.6

Source: Rocznik Statystyeeny, 1975, pp. 55, 116-17

Consequently, in many families the husband continues to be superior in the work career and he remains the principal earner.[16] This also tends to be the norm in choosing the husband. Again in a marriage proposal it is usually the man who takes the initiative and the women consents or rejects. The majority of women, thus, still face a variety of constraints in their progress towards a equal status in the economic and social sphere.[17]

Table 7.23

Average Monthly Income by Sex and Educational Level in Yugoslavia (1986)

Educational Level	*Ph.D.*	*Master's degree*	*Graduate*	*Two year College*	*High-School*	*Primary School*
			(Monthly income in Dinars)			
Men	8646	7316	6731	5168	4383	3355
Women	7364	6053	5584	4281	3683	3155

Skill Level	Highly skilled	Skilled	Semi skilled	Unskilled
		(Monthly income in Dinars)		
Men	4587	3670	3036	2871
Women	3646	2941	2550	2453

Source: Statiscki Bilten, 1169, Beograd, 1980.

The Barriers

In socialist countries, the model of Soviets and Worker's Council through which people's participation in the decision-making processes that govern their life and work was to be ensured, could not be realized due to a variety of factors. The organization of production as well as the governance has remained hierarchical keeping intact the division between those who decide and those who follow the decisions. Under such a situation the family unit plays an important role in the formation of ethico-moral attitudes, in disciplining youth, in lending support to hierarchical relations. Moreover, the fact, that the family unit remains as the consumption unit, keeps the society automized. The members of the family spend a considerable amount of time within their family and this reduces their social activity. The exclusiveness of the nuclear family breeds isolation and individualism. The sphere of family life and household continues to be treated in many aspects as a private sphere of life.

With the abolition of private property a beginning was made towards the elimination of relations in which all the rights belonged to the man as a proprietor, head and provider of the family, the status of the woman being determined by her biological function of maternity. For a further advance towards equality it is essential to work in the direction of integrating the biological reproduction with the overall social reproduction.

It is through the socialization of child care that the roots of conflict between maternity, work and participation in social affair can be removed. Distribution according to need in favour of all children with respect to child care, health care, education *i.e.* placing the care of children in the centre of social concern will help the promotion of a society of equal opportunities, a society in which social roles of men and women become the same. It is the organized effort of men and women that would help accelerate the expansion of socialization of child care and housework. This means a change in the priorities of consumption and priorities of production. Today, the men and women in the socialist countries are not resisting the dominance of externally determined consumption values. For example, in Poland, Gierek's policy of expansion of private consumption and the presumption that woman's prime concern is the home and children was not challenged in the early seventies. As serious contradictions surfaced after about a decade of the pursuit of Gierek's Plan, the people reacted sharply. The working people united to form the independent trade union—Solidarity and pressed with vigour the demand for self-management.

III

Liberation of Women in China

"For over two thousand years until Liberation, the working women were subjected to oppression by the reactionary political authority, class authority, religious authority, and the authority of the husband and downtrodden at the lowest stratum of society ... The establishment of the socialist system in China has eliminated class clause of oppression and exploitation of working men and liberated the masses of women politically, economically and culturally."

In may, 1950 a new Marriage Law was enacted in China. It established the right of divorce for both husband and wife, equal rights to property and equal responsibility for the care of children. It called for families based on a new kind of marriage, one founded on free will with mutual respect. The old practices of bigamy, concubinage, child, betrothal and exaction of money in connection with marriage were prohibited by law.

The All China Democratic Women's Federation took up the task of informing women of their new legal rights and encouraging them to use those rights. The number of divorces skyrocketed in the early fifties. The Federation encouraged women to leave the confines of homes to work in productive labour.[18] The problem was attacked on three fronts, *viz.*, ideology, practical problems and leadership. The political movement and mass campaigns that swept the countryside helped embolden the women and break many a traditional fetter.

Land Reforms

The land reform programme destroyed the landlord and undercut the base of lineage estates. Land was distributed to individuals and women also received their due share. They could even threaten to withdraw their share in the course of divorce. However, individual claim to land often remains more potential than real and women who had little experience in organizing agricultural production held the land in name only. After 1952, when mutual aid teams and co-operatives were organized by pooling land, often times the hold of kinship group was re-established. The women lacking training and skills could hardly attain the leading positions in the co-operative. The fact that teams and brigades often had a kinship base made for the persistence, in some measure, of the age-old discrimination between the sexes in education, in participation in social and political work and in productive labour. Household chore by and large remained the responsibility of the women.

The women in productive agricultural labour earned relatively smaller incomes.[19] This was because they often work a shorter labour day to meet domestic responsibilities, lose work days during menses or pregnancy. In addition women perform tasks that often receive lower work-point evaluation in terms of effort or skill required.

With the beginning of the First Five Year Plan in 1953, the national aim was to improve production, to meet new quotas, and for this to bring women into production. The emphasis on production perpetuated, to a considerable extent, the traditional division of labour between sexes. When jobs were few, women were even encouraged to return to the kitchen.

Cultural Revolution

In the mid-1966 the cultural revolution revived the concern for fighting the tight family authority structure, the hierarchical structure of social deference and obligations between the generations and sexes that hindered political participation. Women were encouraged to engage in study, small group political work and criticism of their families.

In 1972 the women's association was reorganized and became involved in educational projects, family planning and greater participation of women in production, implementation of the principle of equal pay for equal work, increasing the number of women cadres and bringing more women into political activity and study. Birth control methods got actively promoted and increasingly adopted providing alternatives to motherhood as woman's major role. The one-child family ideal was propagated with vigour, and actively supported by the state. Awards and benefits to couples who volunteer to have one child are provided in the form of monthly health care subsidy till the child reaches 14 years of age, grain allocations from infancy equal in amount to those of adults, larger private plots, etc. Special considerations is also given in such respects as housing, medical care, admission to nurseries and kindergarten, while a family with more than two children has to bear an extra tax on income. Infant mortality which was around 120 per 1000 in the 40s has been reduced considerably by vastly increasing the health care facilities and special care of pregnant women and young children. Consequently the burden of child bearing and child rearing is lessening.

Day care facilities for children are provided at the factories. Besides, the neighbourhood committees and the street committees operate nurseries, kindergarten, and medical centres. In the countryside, child care facilities are less adequate. However the grandmothers often help look after the children. Besides, the schedule of farm work being relatively flexible, some adjustments can be made for accommodating the two responsibilities.

To recapitulate, the revolution in China, wiped out within one generation the most glaring aspects of inequality between the sexes. Legal restrictions that bound the women to the family were removed and women were freed from the confines of the home. The village-level hierarchies and the lineage system were attacked but the authority vested in kinship was not effectively broken. In rural China, the traditional division of labour between the sexes was not by and large disturbed. As long as agricultural production demands considerable physical labour, it is not easy to break the traditional work allocation pattern on the farm. Nevertheless women have secured positions in the management of the work collectives and in political leadership (Tables 7.24, 7.25, 7.26), though the number of women on the leading bodies is small. Conscious efforts are being made to involve women in leadership. Women suffer from the handicap perpetuated for centuries as they had not participated equally in production and shouldered any social responsibility.[20] Emphasis is therefore being put on training and preparing a mature women cadre and including such women as watchdogs on the decision-making bodies rather than giving emphasis to having a certain number (quota) of women in leadership.

Women have moved into a number of jobs hithertofore considered to be men's jobs and men are also found in some of the feminine vocations. About 40 per cent of the labour force in China is made up of women. Women have entered all sectors of the economy—industry, transport and communications, buildings, finance. Women work as oil drillers, pilots, and high-tension power line workers. Together with men they take up tasks like operating cranes, driving fork-lift trucks, operating lather, doing welding and so on and the men together with women, work in watch factories, or in hospitals. The proportion of women is larger in the textile and light industry but they make nearly 20 per cent of the work force in heavy industry and mining.

Table 7.24

Women in the Party Committees and Revolutionary Committees in Some Work Collectives in China

Work-Collective	*Percentage of women in the Workfore*	*Party Committee*		*Revolutionary Committee*	
		Total members	*Female members*	*Total members*	*Female members*
East is Red Auto Factory	33	29	3	43	5
Tangshan Rolling Stock Factory	16	21	1	25	1
Textile Machinery Manufacturing—Factory	18	19	1	40	3
Wuhan Sewing Machine Factory	67	10	1	17	2
Foreign Languages Printing House	33	19	3	17	3
Kairan Coal Mine	7	25	2	33	2
Doug Feng Watch Factory	50	17	2	17	3
Red Flag Embroidery Factory	90	3	2	8	5
Manchi Zhai Commune	50*	10	2	29	5
Tianjin Production Brigade	50*	7	1	9	2

* Approximately.

Source: Goldwasser, p. 171.

Table 7.25

Representation of Women in the Chinese Communist Party and Trade Unions

	No. of Full members	*% Women*
Eighth party congress (1956)	96	4.2
Ninth party congress (1969)	170	7.6
Tenth party congress (1983)	195	10.3
Eleventh party congress (1988)		19.0

(Contd.)

	No. of Full members		% Women
Congress of Peking Trade Unions (1973)	2396	Delegates	36
Leading Committee elected at the congress	120	Member	35
Congress of Shanghai Trade Unions (1973)	1598	Delegates	39
Leading Committee elected at the Congress	158	Members	31
Tenth Communist Young League Congress (1978)			25

Source: Goldwasser, p. 177, Kelkar, p. 22

Table 7.26

Proportion of Women among Basic-Level Deputies in China

Year	*Women (%)*
1953	17.3
1968	20.0
1983	22.4

Source : Croll, p. 35

The progress of women in education, acquisition of new skills and entry into new vocations is noteworthy in urban areas. In the social sphere women are freed of many traditional fetters and can exercise their choice in marriage. Marriage does not usually affect their occupation or political activities. The status of a women, which was traditionally determined by her marital position and her husband's status, is now getting more linked to her education and work. In contrast, in rural areas, despite collectivization, the traditional household and clan organizations retain, in certain measure, their material base; private sector of economy exists in the form of private plot and animal husbandry and the household remains in a variety of ways the production unit and consumption unit. As the network of community services is not adequately developed in rural areas, domestic work is still quite demanding and is considered as women's work. Consequently women are valued in terms of their contribution to unpaid labour and reproduction of labour power (sons), and the control of elders on the movement of women in marriage is considerable. Because of the practice of surname and village exogamy women remain temporary members in their natal village and outsiders in their husband's village and both the household and the community give less attention to their education. Despite the new ideology of equality and inclusion of the majority of women in social production, the structural constraints imposed by the household and kinship groups are inhibiting further redefinition of the role and status of women in rural China. It is through the advance in industrialization, urbanization and development of the economic base that the traditional social and economic structures will lose their weight and will make way for further improvement in the status of women.

Conclusion

The changes in the production relations effected through the socialist revolution created conditions that made possible the weakening of the traditional family and disintegration of religious organizations in a short span of time even in a pre-industrial country like China so as to bring women into social production and modern education. The further advance towards equal status is restricted because of the existence of an hierarchical economic and political power structure and the centralization of power in the hands of the bureaucracy and technocracy both under the 'Estatist' model of the U.S.S.R. and the 'self-managed' model of Yugoslavia.[21] The felt necessity for active participation by the mass of working people in the planning and management of the economy and the regulation of the polity and organized efforts towards its actualization will alone pave the way for eliminating the entrenched interests that have grown within the system of state ownership or group ownership and the materialization of self-management that presupposes a new social practice at all stages and levels.

Self-management implies the establishment at the base of the society, of a complex net work of active bodies in which the actual producer plays a decisive role in the decision-making process. Establishment of effective self-management at the enterprise, institution and other work unit levels in intimately bound with the realization of a system of direct democracy which implies a continuous and continuously renewed movement deriving its organizational capacities from within itself rather than a formal system of representation.

Democratization at the work place and the socio-political level and the active participation of the working men and women in managing economic production and socio-political affairs can make possible the change in the social priorities. The production of goods and services of mass consumption will get precedence over the production of special goods like the private car. Full socialization of domestic work and child care will free the women from the narrow confines of the family. At the same time, the role which the family has assumed today as the haven because of the lack of opportunity for effective participation and expression in the public sphere will also change. If the full and active participation of men and women in work makes for creative self expression, the nature of work as instrumental to consumption will not remain so. Such changes in the economic, social, political and cultural spheres will make for further progress on the road to equality between men and women in work and status.

REFERENCES

Heitlinger, Alena, *Women and State Socialism: Sex Inequality in the Soviet Union and Czechoslovakia,* Macmillan, 1979.

Work and Family Life, The role of the Social infrastructure in Eastern European Countries, I.L.O. Geneva, 1980.

Scott, Hilda, *Does Socialism Liberate Women, Experiences from Eastern Europe, Beacon Press, Bosten, 1974.*

Koski, **B.,** *The Situation of Women in Poland* in Critique-11.

——, U.S.S.R. Year book, 1981, Novosti Press Agency, Moscow, 1981.

——, Women at Work, ILO, No. 1/1977, No. 1/1979.

——, Principal Statistical Information on Women in Society of the SFR Yugoslavia, Beograd, 1977. (referred to in the test as 'Women in Yugoslavia').

N. Vishneva-Sarfanova, *Soviet Women: A Portrait,* Progress Publishers, Moscow, 1981.

——, Facts about Poland, Warszawa, 1980.

Jancar, Barbara W. *Women Under Communism,* The Johns Hopkins University Press, Baltimore, 1978.

——, Social Guarantees in Czechoslovakia, Prace, Prague, 1977.

Dodge, Norton T., *Women in the Soviet Economy,* The Johns Hopkins Press, Baltimore, 1966.

——, Poland: Statistical Data, Central Statistical Office, Warszawa, 1981.

Lapidus, Gail Warshofsky, *Women in Soviet Society:* Equality, Development and Social Change, University of California Press, Berkeley, 1978.

Tomsic, Vida, *Self Management and Participation of Women in Development,* A paper presented at the International Seminar on Popular Participation, Ljubljana, Yugoslavia, May 1982.

Croll, Elisabeth, *Women in Rural Development,* the People Republic of China ILO, 1979.

Diamond, Norma, *Collectivization, Kinship and the Status of Women in Rural China,* in Towards an Anthropology of Women edited by Rayna R. Reiter, Monthly Review Press, New York, 1973.

——, China Reconstructs, Vol. XXIX, No. 4, April 1980.

Goldwasser, Jannet and Dowty Stuat, *Huanying: Workers' China,* Monthly Review Press, New York, 1975.

——, Economic Survey of Europe in 1980, United Nations, New York, 1979.

——, Structural changes in the Economies of the European Socialist Countries after the Second-World War, Prague School of Economics, Prague, 1981 (referred to in the text as "Economies of the European Socialist Countries").

——, The Economic Role of Women in the ECE Region, United Nations, New York, 1980.

(Referred to in the text as Economic Role of Women').

——, The Working Women in Peoples' Poland, Ministry of Labour, Wage & Social Affairs, Warsaw, 1975.

——, The USSR in Figures for 1978, Central Statistical Board, Moscow, 1979.

——, The Development of the Czechoslovak Economy, Orbis, Prague, 1974.

——, Demographic Yearbook, United Nations, New York, 1979.

——, Kelkar, Govind, Comparative Analysis of Indian and Chinese Experiences of Indistutianalization of Popular Participation in Development (Mimeographed Paper), 1980.

NOTES

1. In U.S.S.R. (now, the cis) the proportion of women workers with secondary education and above was 76.9 per cent and the corresponding proportion for man was 76.7 per cent in 1976. In Poland the respective proportions in 1973 were 34 per cent for women, 21 per cent for men and about 22

per cent men as against 15 per cent women had completed primary vocational training. In Yugoslavia, among the employed persons in the socialist sector 27 per cent women had completed secondary education the corresponding proportion for men was about 19 per cent (1971). The proportion of men who had attended school for skilled workers was 26 per cent while the corresponding proportion was 15 per cent in the case of women.

2. For example, in Czechoslovakia canteen catering was expanding rapidly when eating places were heavily subsidized by the plant management. Since 1963 the measures taken to put them on a paying basis led to the closure of some canteens and raising of prices in others. In the midseventies only about 17 per cent of the employed people were taking their meals at work places.

3. It is found that for the provision of adequate socialized child care it is necessary to have one adult per five children. In addition some administrative and ancillary work is involved. If this is compared with the average family of two children per women the saving in labour time by socialization of child care (0.3 years) amounts to only about 50 per cent.

   (i) It was noted in Czechoslovakia in the mid-sixties that the annual cost of child care in a creche was KCS 5720 and it was KCS 1500 in a kindergarten. If there were two children in the family aged 2 and 5 the social cost for looking after the children came to 7220 which amounted to about 50 per cent of the mother's salary. The cost to the family is however kept low, there being 85 per cent subsidy in the case of creches.

   (ii) In U.S.S.R., it is reported that the real cost of caring for one child is 400 roubles a year in the kindergartens and 440 roubles a year in the nurseries. The charges made to parents which are determined in accordance with the family income, represent on an average only 18 per cent (for nurseries) and 26 per cent (for kindergartens) of the real costs involved in the care of a child.

4. *(i)* A Czech investigation conducted in 1966-67 of five hundred women holding managerial posts revealed that half of these women did all the housework themselves and about 35 per cent divided it equally with another member of the family. As far as husband's help was concerned 50 per cent of the women said that he helped rarely and 10 per cent said 'never'. They spent on an average three hours daily on housework, one hour on shopping and two-three hours on their children.

   (ii) In another Czechoslovak study carried out in the early seventies it was noted that in 23 per cent of the cases the husbands helped daily in housework, on most days in 12 per cent of the cases, sometimes in 42 per cent and none at all in 15 per cent of the cases.

(iii) In Poland 70 per cent of the married women and 55 per cent mothers bringing up children are employed. For women the working day lasts for 16 to 18 hours. The working women in a textile factory, with one child were noted to devote about eight hours to domestic work. As regards the help from the husband a study carried out by the Centre of Labour Sociology in the early seventies gave the following statistics: six per cent husbands are concerned with washing and dressing their children, three per cent supervise the children's meals, three to six per cent take their children to the creche or to the kindergarten and 15 to 22 per cent take their children for walks.

(iv) A study in Soviet Union (1970) indicated that the husbands help their spouses in housework in about 25 per cent of the cases. It was however noted that among the younger couples the practice of sharing of domestic chores *equally* is tending to gain acceptance and a recent sociological survey noted that one-third young families follow this practice.

5. Women have moved in large numbers into new spheres of activity. For example, among the engineers, women had a share of 14.7 per cent in Poland and as much as 52 per cent in the U.S.S.R., (1977), while it was as low as 1.3 per cent in the U.K. and U.S.A. Among doctors women had a share of 37 per cent in Yugoslavia, 42 per cent in Czechoslovakia, over 70 per cent in the U.S.S.R. While in the U.S.A. the proportion was nine per cent only.
6. The findings of a survey conducted in 1966, in Czechoslovakia indicated that 45 per cent of the women had a negative attitude towards improving their personal skills due to the burden of housework whereas no man faced such a problem.
7. Considerable progress has been made in the representation of women in the political bodies. In U.S.S.R. there were 19 or 2.8 per cent women deputies at the 10th Party Congress (1921) whereas their number at the 25th Party Congress (1976) was 1225 *i.e.*, 25 per cent of the deputies. Women constitute about a third of the members of the Supreme Soviet of the U.S.S.R. and 35 to 40 per cent of the members of the Supreme Soviets of Union Republics and Autonomous Republics. The proportion of women in the communist party increased from 14.8 per cent in 1937 to 19 per cent in 1952 and to 24.7 per cent in 1977. In the Central Committee the proportion of female members was 7 per cent in 1952, it increased to 15 per cent in 1952 and subsequently remained about the same.

In Poland, there were 95 women deputies in the Seym (1976-1980) *i.e.*, 21 per cent of all the deputies. In the people's councils at all levels women account for 28 per cent of the councillors and in the residents self government bodies for more than 30 per cent. In Yugoslavia the share of women in SFRY Assembly, Assemblies of Republics and provinces and commune assemblies was around 15 per cent in 1974. In an advanced Republic like Slovenia their share was 26 per cent. It may be noted that in France women account for only two per cent of the member of the parliament and in Britain, four per cent in the House of Commons while the average in the socialist countries is about 30 per cent.

At the same time the women have not yet reached the top decision making bodies in significant numbers. The number of women holding national ministerial posts, membership of State Council or chairmanship of national assemblies is also quite small (three out of 56 in Poland, and three out of 52 in Yugoslavia in 1976).

8. Investigation in the Soviet Union indicated that the factors that promote women to be in gainful employment are, interest in-work, economic independence and self-respect, to be in the working group, to use one's qualifications and knowledge, to work for the society, to improve income.

9. The immediate post-revolutionary period was characterized by a questioning of the family structure. There were attempts to lessen the importance of the family unit by providing collective forms of life *e.g.*, canteen, collective outings. etc., and by minimizing the educative function of the family through the establishment of institutional facilities. Divorce was made very easy and legal discrimination against the children born out of wedlock was done away with. Both in the U.S.S.R. and Czechoslovakia the family structure got loosened under the impact of the new economic and social relations. But in Poland where agriculture continued to be mainly in the private sphere, less than 20 per cent of the land is in State ownership) and the influence of the Catholic Church quite widespread, the family ideology continued to hold a greater sway.

10. In Czechoslovakia, provision for unpaid maternity leave for a period of one year was made in 1968, the leave period was extended to three years in 1972.

    In Poland, legislation introduced in 1968 and amended in 1972 and 1976 gives a woman the right to a three-year period unpaid leave for looking after her own or an adopted child. The number of women benefiting from this type of leave rose from 50,000 in 1970 to 285000 in 1974. Some women do not take advantage of it for financial reasons. The introduction of a child rearing allowance is under discussion.

11. In Czechoslovakia, child care grants are paid to all women, if they decide to give regular care to their second and additional child. The grant is paid till the child reaches two years of age; the grant amounts to 500 KCS per month for a single child and 800 KCS for twins. At childbirth a grant of 2000 KCS is paid per child (the amount in 1964 was 650 KCS).

12. If the newly weds take the loan for buying or furnishing a flat (upto 30,000 KCS to be repaid in ten years), the loan is reduced by 2000 KCS then the first child reaches one year of age and on the birth of the second and each additional child by 4000 KCS.

13. "Nurseries and kindergartens adhere to standards laid down at the central level concerning hygiene, feeding and the structure of the health and teaching staff. The opening hours of these establishments are arranged so as to enable

the parents to complete their days work."

Provision for the care of children outside school hours is also made. Children can lunch in the school canteen, do their homework or take part in various activities under the supervision of qualified staff. In addition, services like supervised study and holiday camps are also provided on a wide scale.

14. *(i)* In Czechoslovakia for about 12 per cent of the children (0-3 years) creche facility and for 48 per cent of the children (4-6 years) kindergarten facility was available in 1967 and in 1977 the corresponding proportions were 12 per cent and 70 per cent respectively.

(ii) In the U.S.S.R. , creche and kindergarten accommodated respectively 12 per cent and 23 per cent of the children in the respective age groups in 1964. In 1960, a system of integrated pre-school establishments (this provides continuity in the child's social environment) was introduced; subsequently the number of combined establishments increased and the number of separate establishments decreased; precise data on the respective figures of the number of children attending nurseries and kindergartens are not available. In 1977 the number of children attending kindergarten, combined establishments and nurseries was 2.5 million, 9.2 million and 1.0 million respectively, *i.e.,* over 40 per cent children of pre-school age attended a child-care institution.

(iii) In Poland (1974) creche and kindergarten facilities were available only for about 10 per cent and 53 per cent of the children respectively while in Yugoslavia (1976) it was limited to 2.4 per cent (creche) and 11.6 per cent (kindergarten) children only.

15. It was noted that the women's average earnings as a proportion of the men's average earnings worked out to 87 per cent in the U.S.S.R., while the corresponding proportion in Poland and Czechoslovakia was 67 per cent.

In the erstwhile U.S.S.R., research has shown that in the case of 17 per cent of the married couples husband and wife received the same pay, in 25 per cent cases, the wifes' pay was higher (25 per cent married women had more advanced education than their husbands) and in the remaining, the husbands' pay was higher (in 25 per cent cases husbands' pay was one-third higher). It is noted that at the beginning of the marriage, couples often start virtually on par but the husbands acquire more qualifications and advance more while wives make less progress, because of domestic responsibilities.

16. In Czechoslovakia on an average, the husband's earnings made for 48 per cent, the wife's 21 per cent, other earner's four per cent of the total family income in the working class.

17. Note must however be taken of the fact that as women are advancing in their careers, some have established their equal position in the family and they command social recognition and respect. For example, in the advanced republics of Yugoslavia *viz.* Croatia and Slovenia this was noted; as the

women have become economically and socially independent, the men seems to have lost their 'place' in the family and even at a job the women are competing and some are excelling them. The women expressing their new found identity in the 'work' are serious, hard working and are putting considerable effort and zeal in their career. They have divorced their husbands if they find that the husbands are not responsible and have assumed the responsibility as of the head of the family, with inexhaustible strength they are bringing up their child and at the same time putting their best effort into their career. Some women expressed the view that their primary aim is to pursue their work and social interests; they prefer not to marry. They have confidence and poise and can choose men of their liking without getting tied to them.

18. Throughout the 1950's a combination of policies to specifically encourage women to enter social production were introduced and implemented:

    (a) Local women's groups were assigned a major role in encouraging women to take part in social production, overcome their prejudices against working in the fields, acquire and master farming techniques.

    (b) Steps were taken to encourage women—a disadvantaged group in the villages (men had contempt for women's capabilities and women lacked confidence)—by giving them new inputs and new methods of cultivation.

    (c) Training courses were established for leaders of women's groups and production teams.

    (d) Women were encouraged to enter into agricultural collectives in their own right as individual and equal partners with the men. The principle of equal pay for equal work was accepted. Payment for work was directly made to women. This provided not only a measure of economic independence but also served as a means to furthering the individual prestige and authority of women within the household and in the village.

    (e) An important measure designed to enable women to enter social production with a composed mind was the establishment of communal services to reduce the burden of household responsibilities and chores.

    (f) To promote full participation measures to protect the health of rural women were introduced. A network of health clinics was organized to improve the hygiene of child birth and health of mothers and infants. It was stipulated that during menstruation, pregnancy, birth and lactation the work assignment given to women should be suitably adjusted.

    (g) The plan for expansion of production demanded substitution of men's labour power and women's labour (in their eyes and in the eyes of man) became necessary and a valued part of labour force.

    (h) Women were actively encouraged to acquire new skills and techniques.

19. In addition to the work in the collective sector, the tasks of raising pigs and chickens (in the private sector) are normally defined as women's tasks. They often tend the private plots. And the main work *viz.*, the work in the domestic sphere which is very crucial for the largely self-providing rural households (and includes besides cooking, cleaning, washing and child-care, duties like grinding corn, preserving vegetables, sewing etc.), remains unpaid.

20. In rural china, the progress of women in the publiç sphere has been slow, because of their inherent disadvantaged position in the household and kin groups. As sons make permanent contribution to the household and kin groups and support their parents in old age, they get a priority in education and training. The daughters have often to leave the natal community on marriage and hence training of young women in economic and political skills yields little dividends to the local communities. The women, as outsiders in their husband's village, have the uphill task of acquainting with the new community and building up a network of supports if they desire to enter the public field. Besides, they have to shoulder almost the full responsibility of domestic work in addition to the collective and the private work, and hardly have any leisure to participate in the social and political sphere.

21. In the system of self-managed socialism in Yugoslavia there are certain weaknesses *e.g.*, *(i)* With thenegation of central planning and State control the economy is basically regulated via the market; there is the absence of democratic regulation of the national economy as a whole. Group ownership *i.e.*, aspirations of groups have become the carriers of disintegrating tendencies. *(ii)* Success of individual enterprise being subject to the market forces, technocratic and bureaucratic domination persists. *(iii)* There being unequal participation in the decision-making process the interests of the lower strata of the working community do not get proper representation.

8

Indian Women as Foreign Students

General Trends

Nearly 5,250 Indian Women went abroad for study or training during the decade 1975-85 according to the published statistics of Ministry of Education and Social Welfare. Of them Women Students and Trainees (WST) in the fields of Arts and Humanities (A & H) were about 2,100 giving an annual average of about 200. The outflow in A & N constituted 49 per cent of the total outflow during the decade. Year-wise data are given in Table 8.1.

Those who went for study or training in A & H were slightly smaller in number than those belonging to Scientific and Technical fields who went abroad during the same period, the letter category claiming 51 per cent of the total. About five per cent of the total Indian Students and Trainees who went abroad during 1975-85 were women. Roughly six per cent of the total outflow in the S & T category and about 17 per cent of those gone abroad in the A & H category, were women. There were considerable fluctuation in the yearly outflows of Indian WST in A & H. Year-wise, the largest number of Indian WST in A & H, nearly a quarter of the decade total, went abroad in 1978-79. In 1976-77 again an outflow of more than 400 was reported. In all the other years, the outflow ranged from 100 to 200 per annum, the lowest being a little over 100 in the year 1984-85.

Table 8.1

Women Students and Trainees in Arts and Humanities: 1975-85

Year	*Total WST*	*WST in Arts and Humanities*	
		No.	*%*
1975-76	352	195	35.4
1976-77	749	428	57.1
1977-78	283	168	59.4
1978-79	720	497	69.0
1979-80	209	114	54.5
1980-81	281	152	54.1
1981-82	245	115	46.9
1982-83	366	181	49.5
1983-84	640	131	20.5
1984-85	409	107	26.2
Total	4,254	2,088	49.1

An examination of the percentage of WST in A & H gone abroad annually in relation to the total number of WST gone abroad reveals some interesting trends. The percentage of WST in A & H increased steadily from 1975-76 to 1978-79. Thereafter it has been more or less steadily falling with minor fluctuations. The average during the last two years (1983-85) was less than 25 per cent of the total WST gone abroad. Thus there is a noticeable fall both in number and in percentage of WST in A & H going abroad.

Subject-wise Distribution

The fields of A & H have been divided into the following subjects in the Education Ministry publications:

1. Arts
2. Education
3. Commerce & Business Management
4. Banking & Insurance
5. Journalism & Library Science
6. Law
7. Others

The number of WST who went abroad in each of the above subjects is given in Table 8.2.

Table 8.2

Women Students and Trainees in Individual Subject: 1975-85

Subject	*Women Students Trainees*	
	No.	*%*
Arts	687	32.9
Education	180	8.6
Commerce & Business Management	88	4.2
Banking & Insurance	2	0.1
Law	23	1.1
Journalism & Library Science	24	1.2
Others	1,084	51.9
Total	2,088	100.0

Roughly one-third of the Indian WST who had gone abroad belonged to Arts. Education attracted about nine per cent of the total. The proportion of those who went for study or training in Commerce and Business Management was less than five per cent, Over 1000 WST, constituting more than half of the total in A & H, have been classified under "others", details for which are not available.

Comparative Picture *vis-a-vis* Male Student

A comparative picture of men and women students and trainees in individual subjects under A & H who went abroad during 1975-80 and 1980-85 is presented in Table 8.3.

Compared to the outflow of WST during 1975-80, the outflow during 1980-85 was markedly less. The reverse was true in the case of men students and trainees. As a consequence the percentage of WST among the total outflow in the A & H category decreased from about 36 during 1975-80 to about 11 during 1980-85. On the contrary, the percentage of WST among those gone abroad during the same decade in the S & T category increased from about five during 1975-80 to about eight during 1980-85.

Table 8.3

Men and Women Students and Trainees in Individual Subjects: 1975-80 and 1980-85

Subject	*1975-80*		*1980-85*	
	Men	*Women*	*Men*	*Women*
Arts	1,129	424	1,297	263
Education	253	130	263	50
Commerce & Business Management	489	19	2,216	69
Journalism & Library Science	28	14	92	10
Law	87	8	159	15
Banking & Insurance	91	2	36	—
Others	1,784	805	2,276	279
Total	3,861	1,402	6,339	686

Subject-wise also there were some perceptible differences in the directions of movement of Indian men and women students and trainees in A & H who went abroad during the two quinquennia, except in the cases of Commerce and Business Management and Law (the numbers increased for both sexes) and in Banking and Insurance (the numbers decreased for both). In all other cases the number of men among Indian students and trainees who had gone abroad increased, while the number of women who had gone abroad decreased.

The increases in the case of WST that took place in the cases of Commerce and Business Management and Law, however, were almost negligible. For instance there was an increase of 50 in the number of WST gone abroad in Commerce and Business Management, and an increase of seven in Law, during 1980-85 as compared to 1975-80. In all other subjects there was a decline in numbers during 1980-85, the sizable declines being in the case of Arts, Education and in the undefined category "others"

Country of Study and Training

The destination of Indian WST are given in Table 8.4.

Of the WST in A & H who went abroad during 1975-85, the USA attracted the maximum number of Indian WST in A & H amounting to about 32 per cent of the total outflow. In the S & T category, West Germany with about 42 per cent of the total outflow of Indian WST, secured the first position among the different countries.

The number of Indian WST in A & H was much larger than that in S & T in UK, France, Canada, "Other West European Countries" and USSR.

Table 8.4

Country of Visit of Women Students and Trainees in Arts and Humanities: 1975-85

Country	*Women Students & Trainees*	
	No.	*%*
U.S.A.	660	31.6
U.K.	408	19.5
W. Germany	285	13.7
France	138	6.6
Canada	76	3.6
Other West European Countries	413	19.8
U.S.S.R.	39	1.9
Other East European Countries	20	1.0
Australia & New Zealand	11	0.5
Japan	9	0.4
Other Countries	29	1.4
Total	2,088	100.0

A comparison of the number of WST in A & H who went abroad during 1980-85 with the corresponding number who went during the previous five-year period reveals that the largest decrease was in the case of West Germany where the figure registered a fall of 157, the USA and the UK showed decreases of 128 and 70 respectively.

The State of Domicile

The distribution of WST gone abroad by their Indian state of Domicile is given in Table 8.5.

Table 8.5

Women Students and Trainees in Arts and Humanities from Different States: 1975-85

State or Union Territory	*Women Students & Trainees*	
	No.	*%*
Andhra Pradesh	54	2.6
Assam	8	0.4
Bihar	15	0.7
Gujarat	80	3.8
Himachal Pradesh	2	0.1
Haryana	3	0.1
Jammu & Kashmir	1	—
Karnataka	118	5.7
Kerala	626	30.0
Madhya Pradesh	14	0.7
Maharashtra	463	22.2
Orissa	6	0.3
Punjab	28	1.3
Rajasthan	7	0.3
Tamil Nadu	110	5.3
Uttar Pradesh	46	2.2
West Bengal	135	6.5
Delhi	358	17.1
Others	14	0.7
Total	2,088	100.0

Kerala contributed the largest number of WST gone abroad during the decade, Maharashtra came second, and Delhi third. It may be noted that Kerala and Maharashtra also occupied the first and second position in S & T category in 1975-85. A comparison of the figures of WST who went abroad from different Indian states during 1980-85 with the corresponding numbers during the previous five-year period showed the largest decrease amounting to 502 had taken place in the case of Kerala. Maharashtra, the second largest contributor, showed a fall of 93. Only Gujarat, Madhya Pradesh and Orissa showed slight increases. All the other states recorded considerable decreases.

State and Choice of Subject

Subjects of study or training of WST from different Indian states who went abroad during 1975-85 are given in Table 8.6

Out of 687 Indian women who went abroad as students and trainees in Arts, Maharashtra had contributed most. Delhi had the second position and West Bengal, third. In Education also Maharashtra was the largest contributor and Delhi maintained her second position. In Commerce and Business Management, it was Maharashtra again that contributed the maximum.

In the cases of Journalism and Library Science and Law, Maharashtra was again the leading state. In Banking and Insurance, only two WST had gone abroad, and they too hailed from Maharashtra. The undefined category 'others' had over one half of the WST from Kerala, about 15 per cent from Maharashtra, and about 12 per cent from Delhi.

Thus WST from Maharashtra dominated in all the subjects listed under A and H.

DISCUSSION

As the facilities for higher education in India are excellent, and because of the high costs involved, the number of Indian students securing first degrees from abroad is extremely small. The policy of the Government of India has also been to provide foreign exchange only in exceptional cases for graduate study in A and H abroad. However, a fairly large number of Indian students was observed to go to foreign countries every year for postgraduate qualification, particularly in the field of Science and Technology. In general, compared to Indian men, the proportion of Indian women obtaining postgraduate qualifications in both Arts and Humanities and Science and Technology has been small.

What are the subject in which Indian Women students and trainees take postgraduate qualifications and what are the qualifications obtained? Available information in the field of Science and Technology has already been published. The present paper complete the picture with respect to Arts and Humanities.

The field of Arts and Humanities is beset with many difficulties. Some subjects like Education, Commerce and Business Management, Banking and Insurance, Journalism and Library Science, and Law require professional training and experience, and may have a large component of trainees abroad. Neither the number

Table

Subject by State

State	*Arts*		*Education*		*Commerce and Business Management*	
	Number	*%*	*Number*	*%*	*Number*	*%*
1	*2*	*3*	*4*	*5*	*6*	*7*
Andhra Pradesh	33	4.8	10	5.6	—	—
Assam	4	0.6	3	1.7	—	—
Bihar	6	0.9	3	1.7	1	1.1
Gujarat	40	5.8	11	6.1	15	17.1
Himachal Pradesh	1	0.1	1	0.6	—	—
Haryana	1	0.1	1	0.6	—	—
Jammu & Kashmir	1	0.1	—	—	—	—
Kerala	34	5.0	9	5.0	8	9.1
Karnataka	32	4.7	16	8.9	6	6.8
Madhya Pradesh	3	0.4	3	1.7	—	—
Maharashtra	195	28.4	47	26.1	38	43.2
Orissa	1	0.1	1	0.6	—	—
Punjab	17	2.5	5	2.7	—	—
Rajasthan	5	0.8	2	1.1	—	—
Tamil Nadu	39	5.7	17	9.4	4	4.5
Uttar Pradesh	27	3.9	4	2.2	3	3.4
West Bengal	58	8.4	13	7.2	8	9.1
Delhi	186	27.1	32	17.7	5	5.7
Others	4	0.6	2	1.1	—	—
Total	687	100.0	180	100.0	88	100.0

8.6

of Domicile

Journalism and Library Science		Law		Banking and Insurance		Others	
Number	%	*Number*	%	*Number*	%	*Number*	%
8	*9*	*10*	*11*	*12*	*13*	*14*	*15*
2	8.3	—	—	—	—	9	0.8
—	—	—	—	—	—	1	0.1
—	—	—	—	—	—	5	0.5
3	12.5	—	—	—	—	11	1.5
—	—	—	—	—	—	—	—
—	—	—	—	—	—	1	0.1
—	—	—	—	—	—	—	—
1	4.2	6	26.1	—	—	568	52.4
4	16.7	—	—	—	—	60	5.6
—	—	3	13.1	—	—	5	0.5
9	37.5	8	3.48	2	100.0	164	15.1
—	—	—	—	—	—	4	0.3
—	—	—	—	—	—	6	0.6
—	—	—	—	—	—	—	—
3	12.5	—	—	—		47	4.3
—	—	—	—	—	—	12	1.1
—	—	1	4.3	—	—	55	5.1
2	8.3	5	21.7	—	—	128	11.8
—	—	—	—	—	—	8	0.7
24	100.00	23	100.0	2	100.0	1,084	100.0

of exclusive Indian women trainees who had undergone training during the decade 1975-85 in these subjects abroad not the subjects preferred for training abroad by Indian women is available. Since students and trainees cannot be separated for purposes of detailed studies in the publications of the Ministry of Education cited, it is difficult to come to objective conclusions. Want of details regarding over 1,000 women students and trainees classified under "Others" further complicates the situation.* Efforts should therefore be initiated to collect precise disaggregated annual data on Indian women students and trainees abroad to conduct meaningful manpower studies.

---

* Educational qualifications obtained in India prior to departure are also not available.

REFERENCES

Indian Students Going Abroad and Foreign Students in India, 1965-66 to 1974-75, New Delhi, Ministry of Education and Social Welfare, (Studies in Educational No. 4.

Nayar, B.k., Rao C.R.S. and Gupta S.S., Indian Women Going Abroad for Study and Training, Part I, Scientific and Technical Fields.

9

Portraits of Women in Media

The Impact of media on our lives is a point which does not have to be laboured any longer. Radio, Television, film and the printed word reach all of us in this age of information and each strives to perfect its modes of communication to become more effective as a medium. The roles of various media however, have stretched far beyond the supply of information now, because of the outreach, technological sophistication and in that they speak a universal language using familiar cultural symbols to such a large, receptive audience. In effect this gives them the power to create reality. Media is shaped by existing social reality but by the process of selection, interpretation and effective presentation of certain facts it has the power to create reality which is accepted as such by the audience. The power of creating media reality is concentrated in the hands of a few people and their biases and profit motives operate in the creation of a reality which is often distorted but is accepted but as objective and truthful.

Narrowing the focus to one particular medium: Television and the portrayal of women on it, will make this abundantly clear. Government policy aims at support for women in every sphere but this is belied by the way women are represented and portrayed on Television which is state controlled.

Evening after evening we watch and imbibe skewed images of womanhood on TV and these images are incorporated and enacted in our experience of living. The power of the medium ensures compulsive viewing and all our senses are engaged by the images and sounds that are presented to us packed, with emotion week after week, dispensed in a thirty minute capsule known as serials, soapoperas or dharavahiks.

Portrayal of women in advertisements which is patently sexist, either objectifying the women as a sexual toy or which reinforce role stereotypes and of course project her as the inordinate consumer of more and more products has generated some discussion and protest. Not that this has made the slightest difference to the purveyors of dreams which have no point of contact with the lives of most people in the country. 'Victor' vests are still sold on the strength of a sweaty vest of a macho victor and a pretty young thing swooning in the wings. A wife's worth hangs in balance on her husbands's decision to buy her a 'Prestige' pressure cooker. Dreamily desanitised childcare can be viewed pleasurably in every Johnson advertisement. The list goes on ....

The Women's Serials

The phenomenon which merits immediate and detailed scrutiny is the rush of serials which are purportedly 'women's' serials. Suddenly women are a selling subject for serial markets. It is a situation tailor made for profit as one can serve up any tearjerking, dangerouly anti-women pot pourri as a serial which focusses on women and even gathers accolades for toeing the official line of support and concern for women. ....

All that you have to do is to say yours is a serial "no woman can afford to miss" or "Yeh nari hriday ki bhavnaon, uski kashmakash ka sajiv chitran hai" (This is a true picture of the working of a women's mind and heart, of the conflict and stress in her life).

Potentially powerful stories which read quite differently in print (even in English Translations) are reduced to convenient Bombay, popular cinema cliches which reinforce existing myths about women and their character. At the end of an episode replete with dangerously anti-women images and misrepresentation of the feelings of women, the heroine sometimes miraculously overcomes her repression and mouths a few dialogues about the realization of her own power and independence and hey presto! it becomes a women's serial. Women should rightfully be overjoyed at the exposure that their psyche and condition is getting over a medium such as Television. Why then, was I assailed by a feeling of deep disquiet bordering on disgust as each episode ended. Why could I not respond immediately and coherently to the jibes of male friends about the sudden increased visibility of women on T.V. when their comments after a particularly bad episode had the undercurrent of—"women are like this" I knew that they were not engaging sensitively with the issue, their deadened senses were producing formula responses to the Bombay formula images but my own response was also confused.

A Case Study

The extremely insidious psychological impact was most evident to my mind in the recent serial "Kashmakash". Watching T.V., regularly over March-April 87 revealed any number of sexist biases in the portrayal of women in different serials; they were silly, emotional, dependent, almost always in mother; sister, wife role, they were receivers of violence in almost all the serials. Rural women were portrayed in very few serials, if they were peripheral except when their role as mothers was in question. I will however, focus, my reactions around "Kashmakash" and discuss one episode at length, even though almost every frame in each episode of "Kashmakash" needs to be scrutinised for its psychological ramifications for the viewers.

Let me narrate the story of the episode of 30th March 87 as it was revealed in the frames of the serial. It began with the heroine, a convict pleading wildly for mercy but she is sent to jail. There the other women bicker over little things and she shows much self sacrificing nobility in resolving their quarrels thereby attracting the sympathetic attention of the female prison warden who asks about her life. The heroine then tells her story. She was from a poor family where they all needed to work to eat and her sister and she worked in a shoe factory. She met and fell in love with a man during a wedding celebration. She revealed in a conversation with a friend that she wished—"Ab to Pati Kamaye aur Mai Rani Bankar Rahun"—(Now my husband should earn and I should live like a queen).

She married the man and predictably he turns out to be an alcoholic and gambler who merely gave her two children and then showed no further concern for their collective upkeep. There were prolonged verbally violent exchanges between them and she said she would work again because of the children to which her husband responded with—"Kya tu ghar ke bahar niklegi, naukri karegi .... thik hai, meri razamandi bina tu jane ... mar ja, jake", (Will you step out of the house and work, very well, without my consent, now you are your own—you can die for all I care ....).

Then one day she got delayed after work because her friend took her for a movie. As she waited at the bus stop, two men accosted her and snatched her purse. They then reported her to a policeman saying that she was soliciting customers. The policeman, the upholder of morality said, "Shariff ghar ke logon ko barbad karti hai ... sharir bechti hai ... (You ruin men from respectable families ... You sell your body ...). Her attempt to establish her respectability by displaying her 'Mangalsutra' evoked derisive laughter. At the police station she demanded that her father or husband be called. She then discovered that her father would have nothing to do with her because he cannot risk social dishonour because of the other daughters and husband had no interest in her welfare because she was working without his consent.

As if her cup of sorrow was not overflowing already; in prison she receives a letter from her mother that her younger sister had been married to her husband and the mother notes with satisfaction," Jaise Bhagwan Ne Do Betiyon Ko Par Laga Diya ... Vaise hi teesri ko bhi ... (God has fixed two daughters well ... the third should also be settled soon ...).

All this leads to a momentary flash of insight when the heroine observes, "Aurat ki badnasibi ke liye aurat khud zimmedar hai" (Women are responsible for their own misfortunes) .... "Par mai apni taqat pehchan gayi hun" (but I recognise my strength now and will use it to help other women) ... "Ho sakta hai mai apna ghar kho kar shayad unka ghar bacha sakun "(may be since I have lost my home, I'll be able to help save theirs ....).

Even in my narration which of course gets across the bare outline, it is clear that the story relies heavily on an excess of misfortune heaped on a women making her a recognizable type for easy identification. She is a "Bechari"—a poor unfortunate. The story is resolved by making her mouth few words which appear to indicate that she has decided to take no more injustice but in actual fact the language of the serial conveys something quite different to anybody who is receptive to the message. Even those last sentences consist of an oft-repeated almost masochistic cliche—"Aurat ki badnasibi ke liye aurat khud zimmedar hai"—(Women are responsible for their own misfortunes) and—now I'll use my strength to save the homes of other women even though I have lost my own. The serial ends and we have no inkling of how she will concretise her resolve which is surprising in any case because for anybody who has suffered so grievously in her "home" the realization that "homes" can be spurious havens at best is inescapable.

At another level, inspite of being from a working class background she aspires for the middle class trap of wishing to sit at home while her husband earns. The fact that she has to start working again after marriage is treated as something tragic and it is only her mother-hood which prompts her to break barriers of respectability and step out of the Lakshman Rekha" of the home. Because she does so without her husband's permission any thing can happen to her, and it does. The way the camera treats her as she waits on the bus stop is a clear validation of the attitude that she can be victimised, accused of immorality; she is not respectable because she is in a public space and therefore, accessible to men and this violates the claim of her husband over her and he can in all fairness have nothing further to do with her. Her pathetic claim to respectability is her Managalsutra which is treated with derision. Her wild pleading crying, screaming all reinforce the notion that women cannot cope with public life and should obey their husbands, and however horrible stay' at home. Something clicks in all our brains as existing ideas about women are ratified—women, even working class ones who know the value of work and the economic clout it gives dream only of meeting the perfect man who will give them a housebound life of ease and comfort. Once in the marriage which does not turn their dreams into reality, they should suffer in silence and can be constrained to action only for the sake of their children, who are their children alone. Even then, they step out of bounds of acceptable social behaviour at their own peril. If they go and see a film with a female friend they will have to go home alone in the dark where lurk police men and goondas to extract full benefit from their vulnerability and the Mangalsutra as a badge of honour is useless because its wearers are found in homes, not on the roads. Now they can be suitably punished and even turning inwards they can dredge up one emotion of wishing to save other "homes" because theirs is lost forever.

This plethora of messages damaging to women are picked up from one episode. The other episodes abound in similar attitudes where the whole serial speaks the language of subordination of women, cheapens their emotion and energies to mere filmic sentiment, shows them as petty, scheming, unable to live in harmony with other women because of the struggle to hold men and glorifies motherhood. In some episodes as a token, women mouth a few revolutionary nothings. This only serves to create confusion by the conflict between the words and the message of the image. And as always confusion blocks freedom and clarity of thought in the best of minds, making analysis difficult.

Initiatives by Women

This is not a plea for literary writing by women to be scoured only for such stories which are overtly feminist in their perspective for adaptation in T.V., serials which seek to give exposure to women, to redress the enormous harm done by existing portrayals and images. At the current stage of universal awareness about women such an attempt may find itself lacking in popular appeal which is what T.V., depends on. However to let such a serial as Kashmakash go without raising questions about its impact would be inexcusable. Any story whatever its messages stands on its merit and the creativity of the writer in conveying something about the human condition. But to ham up stories which describe women's oppression and suffering so badly that the finer nuances are lost completely, to reduce their plots to convey that the truth about the condition of women is that they are "Badnasib" (unfortunate) and made for suffering, to use the camera against them without empathy, to choose and select only those stories which lend themselves to such reduction and serve it up as "Nari hriday ki bhavanaon ka sajiv chitran" (A true picture of the feelings of women) is definitely objectionable and dangerous. Women must resist being sold in this manner and it is time they took the power of the medium in their own hands to create truth in their idiom or the pressures of the mass market will make their struggle for change increasingly difficult. They must make media work for them and not against them.

10

Women Entrepreneurs as Professional Entities

Introduction

"At first glance, Mrs. Manju Bhattacharya seems a typical Bengali housewife in her white sari and sindhur smeared parting. But instead of discussing the rising prices of fish, Mrs. Bhattacharya prefers a different set of mathematics as she rattles on about production, turnover and costing. Looks are certainly deceptive, for Mrs. Bhattacharya, apart from being a busy housewife is a busier business woman in the midst of having a very enterprising and fast developing fan industry in Calcutta".[1]

"While most other women begin their day preparing breakfast, Mrs. Bharti Mehta prepares to go to her factory at Raknial where she produces armatures of portable tools. Mrs. Mehta received a fair amount of practical training from Nippon Electrical Industries where she had worked for some time and she acquired her administrative knowledge at the Centre for Entrepreneurship Development in Ahmedabad. Mrs. Mehta has 15 employees working for her and she says with great pride, that she has a turnover of Rs. 50,000 every month. Her grand success has enabled her to pay off half of her loan of Rs. 1.6 lakhs from the State Bank of India, in a very short time. She is now planning to expand her factory".[2]

"Jitender Kaur is a post-graduate in zoology. In 1977 she started the Oriental Food and Bottled Products with seed money provided by Delhi Small Industries Development Corporation and raised the rest of the money from the Punjab and Sind Bank. Today her investment is about Rs. 2.5 lakhs."[3]

The three case studies quoted above illustrate a new phenomena in India: the emergence of the women entrepreneur. A decade ago the women entrepreneur was a species almost unheard of, bar an occasional Sumati Morarji to prove the rule. In February 1984, about 700 women entrepreneurs from different parts of the world and all over India attended and participated in the Third International Conference of Women Entrepreneurs organized by the women's wing of NAYE (National Alliance of Young Entrepreneurs) in Delhi, and NAYE estimates that there are approximately 50,000 women entrepreneurs in the country today, running enterprises ranging from management of hotels and computer services to manufacture of garments, processed foods, chemicals, electronics and engineering goods.

The significance of this phenomena is not that Indian women are now participating in the work force in larger numbers than before, but that for the first time women are entering what was hitherto considered an almost exclusively male preserve. It also indicates the growth of a pool of urban based, educated and technically skilled women workers, for though Indian women have always participated in the labour force in large numbers they have been concentrated largely in the rural areas and in low-paid, low productivity, low skilled jobs, whether in the urban or the rural sectors. This becomes obvious from the following figures:

Out of a total female population of 330 m. according to the 1981 Census, approximately 45.9 m. women are main workers and another 20.4 m. are secondary or marginal workers, giving a total of 66.3 m. and a work participation rate of 20.98 per cent[4], as against 53 per cent for males. Of this 58.6 m. or 88 per cent are employed in the rural sector and only 7.4 m. or 12% work in urban areas. Whereas in the rural areas a majority of women, (60.4%), are self employed, in urban areas, most work for wages only 44.2 per cent are self employed. However, the bulk of these are self employed in low income occupations in the informal or unorganized sector and operate on a very small scale, employing either only themselves or family labour, and cannot be termed entrepreneurs, if an entrepreneur is defined as one who shows enterprise, has an eye for opportunity, a willingness to take risks, a commercial acumen and who through her enterprise creates substantial employment for others. For, though the low income women take risks in producing and selling for the open market, their scale of operation is too small to create significant employment for others. Since entrepreneurship as above defined is likely to be exercised largely by educated urban women, this paper is limited to this strata. Though exact estimates are not available it is obvious that the number of women entrepreneurs cannot be very large because educated women on the whole are only 18.58 per cent of the labour force (6th Plan figures), and educated self employed women will be a very tiny fraction of this.

University enrolment figures for 1982-83[5] show that per year, approximately 32,000 women go in for medicine, about 6,000 for engineering, about 1800 for agricultural and veterinary sciences, and 14,000 for law. Though there will be some dropouts, the figures represent the *flow* of women to other professional careers *per year.* Contrast this to the one estimate we have, of 50,000 women entrepreneurs as the *current stock.* The question then arises as to why when women have taken successfully to other professional careers, their entry into the field of entrepreneurship was so late? What is it in the education and socialization of women which has prevented women from taking to business? Conversely, what motivated those who did? What are their backgrounds in terms of age, marital status, caste and class? What circumstances contributed to accelerate the pace of women's entry into entrepreneurship? What role, if any, did government and others play in this acceleration? Why are there so few women entrepreneurs even now? What problems and constraints do they face? What needs to be done to remedy the situation? These are some of the concerns of this paper.

The Traditional Situation

The most basic factor which inhibited women from taking to entrepreneurship till recently was the attitude of society towards a women's role and place in society. These social values and attitudes were reflected in the education and socialization of girls, and in the institutional arrangements of society. Traditionally, a women's reproductive role was considered her primary role and her role as producer secondary, unless, as in the low income classes, economic necessity forced a woman to support the family. This was particularly so in the case of women from the educated, middle and upper middle classes from which most women entrepreneurs are drawn. Coupled with this was the idealized image of the women as one who subordinated self to the family, gloried in motherhood and regarded her husband as god.

Women were socialized into accepting these role definitions, and expectations through an upbringing on stories from mythology, epics and folklore which glorified women who conformed to the ideal image. Thus women were conditioned to sacrifice their own goals and ambitions, deny themselves their legitimate space and surrender any resources which might have contributed to their independence. They were always today to adjust, accept, accommodate and be dependent on men for support. This was hardly conducive to the development of self confidence, initiative or willingness to take risks, characteristics absolutely essential for entrepreneurship.

These values and attitudes also meant that girls were often given less education than boys, and even when girls were educated upto school leaving or beyond, the aspirations of the parents and even of the girls themselves were lower both as to educational attainments and future prospects. For a young girl marriage and children were considered the only life long activity and education was imparted either to make her a better wife and mother or to secure a better husband, since husbands preferred educated wives.

These attitudes reflected too on the courses and curricula offered to women, these were not designed to equip girls with specialized training for a job or career. If employment was at all considered for a women, it was seen merely as a temporary occupation till marriage. This conditioned not only women's own aspirations but also their judgment of their capacities, choice of occupations or training. It also coloured the attitudes of all who had an influence on this choice parents, teachers, heads of schools and training institutions, employers and policy makers.

Compounding these social disabilities were the economic constraints faced by women. To start a business venture, initial risk capital is essential. Traditionally women did not own any property in their own name, apart from their 'streedhan', which could be mortgaged or used as collateral to raise money; nor did they have any independent sources of income. Access to institutional capital, either from money-lenders or banks was out of the question as they would reject outright any women's ventures as unworthy or risky. Male relatives or friends would not consider financing a woman's venture either.

Over and above the attitudes specifically inhibiting to women, were the attitudes engendered by a stagnant, non-expanding economy which made *all* job seekers, men and women, prefer safe, secure, wage employment, however poorly paid, to self employment involving risks and venture into uncharted areas. In sum, both by education, socialization and economic circumstance, women were inhibited from venturing into entrepreneurship.

"The Old Order Changes"

Today, fortunately, the scene has changed. Women entrepreneurs, though still very few in number, are successfully operating ventures with investments ranging from Rs. 25,000 to Rs. 5 lakhs and employing from 10 to several 100 employees. Though many have started ventures using women's traditional skills in cooking, stitching, knitting etc. and have set up units manufacturing processed foods, readymade garments or offering beauty care services etc., there are others who have gone into very non-traditional fields, using diverse technical skills and are competing with men successfully. Thus, there are women operating shipping and transport concerns, hotels, manufacture of switch gears, electronic tools, radio and T.V., parts, chemicals and pharmaceuticals, *et al.*

(i) Characteristics

There are no definitive studies to show the age, marital status, educational and class/caste, backgrounds of the women who have taken to business as a profession, but some analysis done by an entrepreneurship development programme[6] shows that a majority of the women selected for training as entrepreneurs as well as those already established, are graduates and post graduates and only about 30 per cent are high school passed. In terms of economic backgrounds, most are from the middle class, with a few from the lower middle and a few from the upper middle class. Many belong to families with a business background. Most often it is married women with grown children who take to entrepreneurship rather than unmarried girls or young married women because their domestic responsibilities have eased.

The same programme reports that women entrepreneurs are less aggressive and more emotional and tend to get emotional involved in situations where men would not, but with experience learn to be more objective. They also do not take as many risks as men do, especially in the initial stages. Their projections of capital costs, business opportunities and sales are very much more realistic and sometimes very low. Though this prevents an ambitious expansion, it also prevents disappointment resulting from over estimation. Finally, women who succeed do so because of strong family support in the form of finance, business know-how and freedom of movement.[7]

(ii) Motivation

What motivates women to take to business?

A study by the Center for Entrepreneurship Development Ahmedabad[8] classifies women entrepreneurs into three categories, *viz.*, chance entrepreneurs, forced entrepreneurs and created entrepreneurs. Chance entrepreneurs are women who have gone into business just by chance, without any preparation and due to fortuitous circumstances, in contrast to forced entrepreneurs where women were forced to take to business because a husband or father died and did not leave an heir. Created entrepreneurs are those who underwent training and planned to start business as a career.

Motivation to take to business is either economic compulsion, desire to utilize spare time and make money (these women usually start a small industry in their home or nearby) or a desire to take up a challenging task. Those who have technical education are from the middle class and have capacity and financial means are highly motivated to go into non-traditional areas in business and industry. There are others who have wanted to go into business but could not due to family responsibilities, and lack of technical expertise or money. Once these pressures have eased they are highly motivated to go into training, use all government incentives and start work. These women are the largest in number and from the ordinary middle class. Women coming from industry or business backgrounds have a natural advantage and flair. But the prime motivating factor in all, is the desire for economic independence and the need to prove oneself through overcoming a challenge.

(iii) Factors of Change

A number of factors have contributed to unleashing women's potential in the last decade. One of the most important is the tremendous expansion of education opportunities for women. Female literacy has steadily gone up to 24.8 per cent in 1981 as against 18.69 in 1971. Even amongst literate women, the per cent of women at various educational levels has gone up between the two census periods as shown in the Table below:

Percentage Distribution of Female Literates by Education Levels

	1971	*1981*
Graduates and above	1.35%	2.96%
Matric and high school	7.13%	12.48%
Technical Diploma	0.16%	0.29%

Even in higher education there has been a spectacular growth in the number of women enrolled. In the past 30 years or so, the enrolment of women has gone up by more than 20 times,[9] while the proportion of women to men has increased about three fold during the period. In 1981-82, there were 40 women per 100 men compared to 14 in 1950-51. As a percentage of total enrolment, enrolments of women in higher education has increased from 22.7 per cent in 1971-72 to 28.5 per cent in 1982-83. The number of colleges meant exclusively for women has gone up by nearly 27 per cent over the period 1974-75 to 1982-83 and in 1982-83 there are 643 colleges for women alone.

Significantly, there has been a steady increase in enrolments of women as a proportion of total enrolments in the faculties of medicine, agriculture, law, commerce, engineering, technology and vet. sciences, with the faculty of commerce registering the maximum increase from 3.6 per cent in 1971-72 to 15.0 in 1982-83.[10] The figures speak for themselves about women moving into non-traditional education and explain the increase of women in business. With education has come confidence and motivation to use one's potential. The general spread of education has also aided the process, so that parents are now willing to give girls an education equal to that of boys, and are more willing to let them take up professions and to pursue a career.

This last is, at least in part, due to inflation and economic pressures, which has forced society to reassess women's roles. Inability to make both ends meet has forced women, especially in the lower middle classes to enter the workforce, often at the initiative of parents and husbands. Parents realize that an economically independent daughter can offer them security in old age, as much as boys used to traditionally. Economic pressures have also accelerated male migration from villages to towns and from India, abroad, forcing parents to turn to daughters for support. The paths trailed by women leaders in various fields, most notably by Mrs. Indira Gandhi, has also helped change attitudes towards women's capabilities.

A third factor, apart from education and inflation which has helped women to take to entrepreneurship, is planned development. With acceptance of planning it became evident that if development was to be accelerated, the economy could not afford to ignore the potential for contribution by half the population: Hence efforts were made to involve women in the development process. Also, creation of employment came to be one of the key goals of planning, and since the potential for creation of new employment by the organized sector was very low, due to its very low rate of growth (only 3.4 per cent p.a.) the emphasis from the 5th Plan onwards came to be on promoting self employment, including self employment of women. Self employment for women was promoted on the additional ground that it enabled them to combine better their dual roles of home maker and producer.

Two developments contributed greatly to this focus on women in the planning process. The U.N. declaration of 1975 as the International Women's Year and 1975-85 as the Women's Decade, can be considered to mark a watershed in matters pertaining to women. All over the world it brought into sharp focus women's problems and needs as well as their potential. Debate and research led to a re-examination of women's roles in society and in development and to a demand for measures which would help them realize their full potential and so contribute to society. Action was initiated on several fronts, but most notably on health, education and employment, by national and international, government and non-government agencies.

The focus on women coincided with changes in development theory, which now postulated that a trickle down of benefits of the planned process to the poorest and weakest sections of society could not be presumed and that specially targeted programmes were necessary along with measures to raise the rate of growth. Women were considered on such disadvantaged group to whom special attention needed to be paid.

Role of Government

The Government began its efforts to promote women's self employment around 1978 with a series of measures which included both skills training and provision of services and facilities in the area of credit, material supply, marketing, product development etc. In 1978, the new Industrial Policy Resolution for the first time recognized women entrepreneurs as a special group needing support and assistance. Several government and non-government organizations launched vocational training and entrepreneurship development programmes for women. While the first concentrated on building up skills in particular occupations like catering, designing, printing and electrical assembly, the second was concerned more with motivation, developing entrepreneurial aptitudes and giving the know-how for starting a new business or industry. The Kerala Government was perhaps the first to start a full fledged Women Industries Programme in 1978 with a women officer in charge. Apart from training programmes it offered a number of incentives to women to start new ventures, such as exemption from sales tax for six years from date of commencement of production, marketing assistance, government participation in shares of new ventures, subsidies towards staff salaries, equipment purchase and rent of premises etc. As a result, by 1984, 619 units have been organized by women: 123 industrial co-operative societies, 421 proprietary concerns, four point stock companies, 33 partnership firms and 32 ventures by charitable institutions.

It would be impossible to describe here in detail the various entrepreneurship development programmes that have been initiated, but I will mention a few of the major agencies that are working in the field. The Small Industries Service Institutes (SISI) of different states run motivational training and entrepreneurial development courses and also undertake follow-up activities. The State Bank of India, and various other banks, the Small Industries Development Organization (SIDO), the Centre for Entrepreneurship Development, Ahmedabad and the Entrepreneurship Development Institute of India, Ahmedabad, the National Institute for Entrepreneurship and Small Business Development, Delhi, all run ED programmes for women. The Small Industries Extension Training Institute Hyderabad (SIET) does entrepreneurship motivation development programmes for trainers of promotional agencies and also entrepreneurial motivation development programmes for potential entrepreneurs. It has run 62 programmes so far. The Central Social Welfare Board, the Directorate General of Employment Training (DGET), Ministry of Labour, Government of India, All India Handicrafts Board and the Khadi and Village Industries are also involved in vocational training for women.

Typically, these entrepreneurship development programmes (EDPs) are of about three months duration and cover subjects like entrepreneurial qualities, opportunity guidance, products selection, sources of information, procedures for setting up a unit, schemes of assistance, market survey techniques, achievement motivation, costing and cost consciousness, production planning and control, taxation and budgeting, and effective communication. It includes factory visits, practical in-plant training and project report preparation. Many ED programmes give follow through assistance till a women actually sets up a unit. Thus they recommend the women entrepreneur for a bank loan, and arrange for technical advice if necessary.

There is no all-India data on the number of women who have undergone EDP training, nor of the impact of these programmes in terms of the success or failure rate in terms of women actually setting up and running an enterprise over time, nor any analysis of their background in terms of class and education, the products selected and motivation. This is one major area which future research needs to address.

Disabilities and Constraints

Though efforts have been made, women entrepreneurs still face a number of disabilities and constraints, which are partly due to the fact of being a women and partly general to all trying to set up a new venture in a controlled economy; are partly attitudinal and partly physical.

(i) Attitudinal Barriers

There is an entrenched belief that women are not bread winners and what they do is supplementary activity, and that they should therefore take up those kinds of activities with which they are traditionally familiar such as making pickles, papads, doll-making, knitting etc. Also that they should run such units at home and this generally means run a cottage industry. Since they are conceived to run the business as a pastime or a spare time activity it is presumed that they lack seriousness and commitment.[11]

This attitude is reflected in statements made by even serious policy makers. I quote from the speech of Mr. N.D. Tiwari, then Minister for Industry and Labour, giving the valedictory address at the 2nd International Conference of Women Entrepreneurs in 1981:

"While there is no basic difference in the fundamental factors making for entrepreneurs, there are some special disabilities which particularly effect women coming to the fore to take up self employment opportunities or emerging as entrepreneurs. These relate to questions bearing on how to choose the right product and the skills needed to develop new products, the development of appropriate technology usable in working conditions within the home, the development of viable hand held tools which increase productivity and reduce drudgery etc. Considering the multiple roles that women will *continue to shoulder at home and for the family, any technology framework, especially intended for them must reckon with the fact that the home itself will have to be the work place for a large number of them engaged in self employment.* I am sure that in this complex task our scientists and technologists would engage themselves in order to devise suitable productivity-increasing and fatigue-reducing technology and tools" (emphasis mine).

In many instances, agencies promoting women's entrepreneurial development identity certain projects as suitable to women and believe women cannot set up every type of industry, *i.e.*, there is stereotyping of attitudes of what women can do.

Also, though it is true that many times women entrepreneurs are only fronts to get the various concessions in credit etc., given to them, and it is actually the men who run the business, it is also true that if a women receives any assistance for running a business, it is immediately construed as the man actually running the business.

Society's lack of confidence in a woman's ability is also reflected in reluctance by the family to finance a women's venture; in a closer scrutiny of her application for assistance by financial, industrial and government organizations; and in comparatively harsh guarantee terms by banks in sanctioning loans. Often a women must produce a man guarantor before a bank is satisfied. While the more educated high level staff of promotional agencies are helpful to a women entrepreneur, it is difficult for her to cope with the lower staff who refuse to accept women in the role of entrepreneurs. Social and familial disapproval of contact with members of the opposite sex, which is inevitable if a women is to set up business, also inhibit women from going into business. Not only is she unable to mix freely with professional peers, but is also unable to resort to bribes or socializing which a man may do to get things moving in a controlled economy.

(ii) Other Constraints

Due to her many responsibilities a women has less time than a man to spend on the arduous legal and procedural formalities that have to be completed before setting up a business. There are at least 7-8 major agencies involved in permissions at a minimum, and as many as 27 in some cases, for obtaining suitable industrial sheds, power connections, various licences and registrations, loans and raw materials. To make matters worse there is also a lack of information about facilities available, procedures to be followed, raw material sources etc. Women also lack expertise in identifying viable products, in formulating a credit worthy project, or in marketing, accounting and management.

The lack of a single agency which can be approached for all assistance, and for guidance; the lack of training facilities in management, production and marketing; and the absence of nodal points in various administrative ministries to deal with problems of women entrepreneurs, all add to her problems. Further, women are seldom included in trade delegations or exhibitions abroad and thus are not exposed to new technological developments, or new markets.[12]

And all these difficulties still prevail after six years of government effort on behalf of women.

"We Shall Overcome"

But there are glimmerings of hope and these are that women entrepreneurs have at last decided to help themselves. To fight stereotypes, negative attitude and other problems, as well as to provide support services, women entrepreneurs have begun to organize themselves into professional associations.

In Karnataka, women entrepreneurs have formed AWAKE (Association of Women Entrepreneurs of Karnataka) to lobby for special incentives, amongst them five per cent reservation of industrial land and sheds, subsidy on project reports and know how investment and relaxation of margin money requirements. They have begun a systematic identification of women entrepreneurs so as to enlarge their community. They have succeeded in getting a special women's cell set up in the Technical Consultancy Organization of Karnataka (TECSOK).

The National Alliance of Young Entrepreneurs has set up a Women's Wing which organized the International and National Conventions of women entrepreneurs but unfortunately has done very little constructive follow-up work, such as identifying investment opportunities, development of management and industrial production capabilities, getting better access to capital, infrastructure, and markets; taking up grievances with appropriate authorities, exposing members to domestic and world markets by sending delegations, enabling their participation in exhibitions and fairs etc.; and lobbying in the press and parliament; all, activities which they had mandated for themselves, but not achieved.

A new offshoot of this organization is the Indian Council of Women Entrepreneurs in Delhi which was set up only this year. It is too early to say whether they can rise to the challenge.

Desiderata

What more needs to be done?

(1) The first and most important task remains changing attitudes, of girls and women themselves, and of parents and society towards women's roles and duties. Both, women

themselves, and society at large, need to gain confidence in women's abilities to tackle non-traditional work. This can be done through the formal education system as well as through public education:

In schools and colleges, guidance services could be set up to offer information to women on training opportunities, job opportunities and facilities and incentives available for women entrepreneurs. These centres could, through counselling sessions, make young girls understand the implications of a decision not to take up a career, or to leave the employment market mid career. They could also arrange for meetings and group discussions with successful women entrepreneurs both to motivate the girls as well as for guidance. For such women as have left the employment market, these centres could provide guidance for re-entry.

So far, the vocational content at school leaving stage is designed purely with wage employment in mind. This needs a review to see how entrepreneurship can be encouraged by modifying the content. Curricula can be reoriented to include instruction in practical application, *e.g.* in biology and chemistry teaching, a course could be included on how to set up pathological laboratories, or how standard pharmacological material can be produced. Agricultural universities and Home Science Colleges could introduce a course on the economics and management of food processing, dairying, sericulture or poultry units.

A well co-ordinated public education campaign using all the media, could go a long way towards changing social attitudes towards women entrepreneurs. The media could carry interviews with women entrepreneurs, feature success stories, give information on facilities and incentives available, etc. Favourable public opinion regarding women entrepreneurs will result also in the evolution of an institutional framework to create opportunities for women.

(2) To enable more effective designing of training and support programmes for women entrepreneurs, research is needed on the background, motivation and attitudes of women who take up entrepreneurial activity. Also necessary is careful monitoring

and evaluation of existing training programmes and facilities to highlight reasons for low rate of utilization of incentives and facilities, or to gauge the success rate of training programmes, so that they can be adapted to felt needs.

Simultaneously, experimentation must continue on the most effective ways of delivering support services to women in the area of credit, marketing and product development given that women have different problems and needs from men.

(3) Promotional agencies must build up a shelf of project profiles, suitable for women so that much of the technical spade work is done for them. In building up such a shelf of projects, the link between national welfare programmes for women and the possibilities for women entrepreneur meeting these programme needs can be kept in mind.

To expose women entrepreneurs to new technological development at home and abroad, as also to expose them to new markets, women entrepreneurs should be included in national and international trade fairs, and delegations.

(4) Finally, women's professional organizations need to become more active on behalf of their members, both for advocacy and technical support, providing the kind of services mentioned earlier. They could also offer fellowships to young women graduates to do business administration, or entrepreneurs development training; or to mature entrepreneurs to improve their skills by attending these course.

One looks forward to the day when the women entrepreneur will no longer be a rare hot-house specie, but as common as the hardy hibiscus.

REFERENCES

1. "Lady with the Fan" by Sandhya I. Gupta in "Meet Your Entrepreneur", column of *Financial Express,* December 31, 1979.
2. "Success Story" by Anuradha Chowdhry, *Indian Express,* August 28; 1981.
3. Case Study in "Credit for Self-Employment of Women", Pushpa Sundar, Ford Foundation Discussion Paper, May 19.
4. 6th Plan figures put the work participation rate at 23 per cent for females.

5. University Grants Commission, Annual Report 1982-83. Appendix XXIX, p. 229.
6. Run by the Entrepreneurship Development Institute of India, Ahmedabad.
7. See "Women Entrepreneurship" by the Centre for Entrepreneurship Development, Ahmedabad, in Report of the 3rd International Conference of Women Entrepreneurs 1984. NAYE, Delhi.
8. *Ibid.*
9. In 1982-83, the estimated enrolment in universities was 893,000 as against 40,000 in 1950-51. UGC Annual Report 1982-83.
10. *Source:* UGC Annual Report 1982-83, Sec. 12.
11. See "We Dream Dreams and Ask Why Not?", Mrs. Madhura Chatrapathy in Report of 3rd International Conference of Women Entrepreneurs, 1984, NAYE Delhi.
12. "Women Entrepreneurs in a Progressive World." Manorama Vaid in Report of the 3rd International Conference of Women Entrepreneurs, Delhi, 1984 NAYE.

11

Women Managers and Modern Management A Study of Japan's Corporate Sector

Japan has had a relatively high proportion of women in the labour force since at least the early part of this century. The main shift from the early part of the century to the 1970s was the steady movement of working women from the status of family worker to wage earner.[1] Women now constitute 39.7 per cent of the labour force. Although the transition from family worker to wage earner continues, 20 per cent of women in the labour force were still counted as family workers in 1986 [1].

Less than a century ago, Japan's economy was overwhelmingly agricultural, and women worked alongside men in the fields. In the early stages of industrialization, women were sent to work in the textile industry and other light industries; they formed the absolute majority of factory workers through the 1920s [2]. Later, women were heavily utilized in the war economy that propelled Japan to a higher level of industrialization, during the 1930s and 1940s. Even in the prewar period, small numbers of women with relatively high education also worked in various kinds of white-collar occupations.

Virtually all young women in postwar Japan join the labour force after they complete their schooling. They work for several years until marriage, and often continue until their first pregnancy.

Over ninety per cent of Japanese women marry before the age of 35, and the overwhelming majority of married women also become mothers. Compared with most other countries, there is astonishing uniformity in the age range within which marriage and parenthood take place. Fertility is also highly controlled, with a low illegitimacy rate and an average number of children per family that is now well below replacement [3].

As postwar Japan developed into a major industrial power during the 1960s, the nonworking wife became a status symbol of economic success. What had once been a luxury of elite women was now within reach for a growing segment of the middle and working class. There arose a cultural ideal of the middle-class, white-collar, salaried man, working in a large company, whose wife devoted all her time to her home and the rearing of her children. Such women were expected to utilize their education and skills in managing the home, and were given substantial control over the household economy [4].

Initially, there may have been some economic advantage to this arrangement, in that the full-time mother closely supervised the education of elementary-school children and thus gave them an edge in the meritocratic educational system that determines the social status of the next generation. As the educational competition intensified, however, families shifted to outside tutors and commercial cram schools, and the mother's role became simply to provide emotional support and encouragement to the studying child. The nonworking wife thus became primarily a status display for middle-class households.

Despite its importance as a cultural image, the ideal of the nonworking wife has never represented an actual life-style for the hundreds of thousands of women who participate in the operation of family businesses. During the 1960s and 1970s, it became common for housewives to do piecework at home, in order to supplement the family income, while maintaining the image of the nonworking housewife. Over the past decade, however, married women have been returning to the labour force outside the home more openly, and at present, half of all married women work [5].

Married women who return to the labour force after a break in employment are usually employed in lower-status positions than those they occupied before marriage. Such women are generally classified as part-time workers, who have no employment security, no opportunity for advancement, and no fringe benefits, as opposed to the "permanent" or "regular" workers, who enjoy all of these advantages. About eleven per cent of all employees, and 22 per cent of all women employees, fall into this category. In the past 20 years, the number of part-time workers has tripled, and their proportion of the labour force has doubled. The trend is much stronger for women, who by 1985 constituted 70.7 per cent of all part-time workers. The number of women part-time workers is six times what it was 20 years ago, and their proportion of the female labour force has nearly tripled [1].

Japan has a double-peaked (M) curve of female employment by age, with the overwhelming majority of young, unmarried women in the labour force, a drop in labour-force participation during the early years of marriage and childbearing, and a gradual return to the labour force of growing numbers of older, married women. The bottom of the M has gradually been rising, but is still much lower than in the United States. Because of this demographic pattern of female labour-force participation, coupled with the reality that most women cannot return to the same type of job they left, relatively few women remain in a career track long enough to attain a management-level position in a large corporation.

Employment and Promotion in Large Organizations

The barriers against placing women in managerial positions in large companies stem not only from family ideals in the larger society but also from the strictures of the permanent employment system, another cultural ideal that finds its major expression in large corporations.

In both the public and the private sector, large organizations in Japan hire only entry-level white-collar employees and expect to retain them until retirement in their mid-fifties. Incoming, permanent, white-collar employees are generally employed fresh out of school, with no previous work experience. Management-track employees normally have four-year college degrees, but no specialized graduate training. New employees are given considerable in-company training during their first year on the job. Thereafter, they are moved around to various parts of the company to develop their knowledge and skills and receive continuing in-service training over the years.

Most companies would prefer to send an employee for graduate training, if it becomes necessary, rather than hire someone who already has obtained it on his own. In effect, the company grooms employees for managerial positions by providing a wide range of internal career-development opportunities. To a certain extent, all career employees in a hiring-year cohort receive the same opportunities, but specific assignments are made on the basis of the company's view of each individual's potential.

Virtually all promotions are internal, and are carefully graded by seniority. Thus, after about eight years of service, all permanent employees who entered the company in the same year become eligible for promotion: all attain the rank of *kakaricho,* although some are placed in more-important posts than others. Most will eventually receive a second promotion in rank to *kacho,* about five to six years later. Only a small proportion of these will later become *bucho,* or department heads. The highest-rank promotions are given to people near or even past the formal retirement age. The situation is usually managed so that no one from the same age cohort and rank who is not promoted remains in service.

The Japanese system of organization and management features a narrow span of control with an average of 5—15 people under one direct supervisor. The consequent abundance of supervisory positions, plus the practice of foisting excess managers off into lower-ranked subsidiaries, makes it possible to provide sufficient positions in the main administrative ranks for the entire age cohort.

Large Japanese bureaucracies, both corporate and governmental, have a relatively standardized rank structure of administrative levels, as shown in the diagram. All persons at the rank

Chairman of the Board *(Kaicho)* President *(Shacho)* Managing Directors *(Semmu)* · Vice Presidents *(Fukushacho)* · Board of Directors *(Rijikai)*	Corporate Level
Plant manager or Branch manager (Kojocho) (Shitencho) Department head *(Bucho)* Section chief *(Kacho)*	Administrative Level
Subsection chief *(Kakaricho)* Ordinary employee *(Shain)*	Operating Level

Japanese management levels. Ranks above plant manager or branch manager are considered to be corporate management; section chief to plant manager, administrative-level management. Subsection chiefs are not considered part of management, but may have direct supervisory responsibilities. The latter distinction is related to union membership, which generally includes all permanent employees below section chief.

of section head *(kacho)* or above are considered to be managers who participate in decision making. Management studies sometimes also include the sub-section-head level *(kakaricho)*, the first supervisory-level position, from which appointments to section head are made.

Virtually all employees are rotated within the company at about three-year intervals. Although they fall at the same rank level, these assignments can vary considerably in the amount of responsibility and opportunity they provide. This means that the actual managerial responsibility a person is given may not be reflected in formal rank or even in compensation, which is heavily determined by rank and seniority. At the same time, the range of experience an employee accumulates and the opportunities to develop and display one's skills weigh heavily in the employee's future placement in a developing managerial career.

The seniority-based promotion system creates an attractive and predictable management career track for permanent employees. It is precisely this package that makes white-collar, entry-level positions in large corporations and government among the most prized commodities in the society. This, in turn, fuels incredible competition for entry into the relatively small number of elite universities from which the major corporate employers and the national government hire their permanent employees.

In the private sector, virtually all who acquire these coveted entrylevel positions with a guaranteed promotion ladder are men. Their secure promotion opportunities are preserved, however, primarily by the hiring of large numbers of educated women to fill out the bottom of the employment pyramid at the white-collar rank of ordinary employee.

Young, single women are hired with the expectation that they will "retire" into marriage and motherhood within a few years without being promoted to a higher rank. Because the company does not intend to promote these women, they are often hired at lower educational levels (high school or two-year rather than four-year degrees) or from lower-ranked four-year colleges than are men employed by the same company. The forced retirement of female employees is often helped along by management's urging young, white-collar employees to marry at the appropriate age, preferably to an eligible person in the same company. When two employees marry, nepotism rules are invoked; and, of course, the wife is the one who retires. Although it is against the law to force a woman to retire because of marriage or pregnancy, nepotism is an acceptable reason. Personal social pressures effectively eliminate most of the remaining young women from the white-collar managerial pool soon after they marry.

Until recently, women have generally co-operated with this system. Families traditionally have encouraged women to get the type and level of education that will equip them to marry managers, rather than to become managers themselves. Although the competition for university entrance is open and meritocratic, women still do not compete in great numbers for entry into the elite co-educational institutions. When they do enter, they tend not to go into the "male" disciplines of economics, law, and engineering, from which companies are more likely to hire. Yet there are some eligible women with the same qualifications as the men; and in some cases they are hired for entry-level positions in large corporations.

Japanese Management Culture and Women

Much has been made of Japan's unique managerial culture as another barrier to women. Japanese white-collar employees are expected to work long hours, and to be available until late at night when there are special work demands. Women members of a work group are also expected to stay late when the work requires it. They may make excuses to leave early, which the men could never do, but this is considered evidence of their weaker commitment to the company. Legal restrictions on women's night work have recently been removed, so this can no longer be used as a reason to exclude women from managerial positions.

Japanese managerial style also mixes work and play to a greater degree than is found in other countries. Co-workers are expected to socialize together regularly after work, which often means bar-hopping until late a night. Managers take their subordinates drinking in order to break down the status barriers an permit employees to speak more freely about problems at work and at home. Some women are accepted as full co-workers and invited to join in these activities. Although evening socializing in small restaurants and bars remains heavily male oriented, it is quite possible nowadays for women to participate as part of the group.

The problem thus is not so much an absolute sex barrier as it is a matter of time commitment and personal style. A married women with home and family responsibilities in the evening would be very hardpressed to meet these work demands. A single women or one whose husband had similar work hours could do so more easily. A mother with young children at home could maintain such a managerial life-style only if she had resident child care. Many women would not be comfortable with the evening socializing required of Japanese managers; some men do not like it either, and it also affects their careers.

Another important aspect of Japanese managerial culture is a consensus-oriented decision-making style that aims to avoid conflict after the decision is made by anticipating resistance and negotiating before hand. This encourages a managerial style based on teamwork, and leader who listen and are sensitive to the feelings of others. Ironically, the qualities required of good Japanese male managers are the same qualities that are often held in American management research to be feminine characteristics disadvantageous to success. (In fact, when Japanese managers complain that they have difficulty finding American men who can fit into their overseas operations, the authors have recommended that they try American women.) There is thus no inherent reason why Japanese women would have difficulty handling the decision-making aspects of management, given similar opportunities to develop their skills in the work group. Even in the home, Japanese women are expected to be competent managers and good negotiators, using a similar style of consensus decision-making.

Utilization of Women in Large Organizations

A new equal employment opportunity law, which went into effect on April 1, 1986, is intended to improve the promotion opportunities of women employees. Unfortunately, it has weak enforcement provisions and does not effectively address the problem of differential hiring. It has, however, prompted some new research on the actual status of women in large organizations.

Large firms

A 1986 survey of 321 large firms by the Labour Administration Research Institute found that 79.9 per cent of the firms professed to treat men and women equally with regard to promotion, and that the larger the firm, the greater the support for women's promotion opportunities [6]. This is a substantial increase from a 1984 study by the Women's Bureau, in which only 56.3 per cent of companies reported that they offered promotion opportunities to women [7]. In the more recent study, however, only 1.2 per cent of the companies surveyed had any women above the rank of division manager *(buncho)*. Just 4.1 per cent of the companies had women up to the level of division manager, but about one-fifth (21.6%) had women in positions up to section head *(kacho)*, and slightly more (22.8%) had women in the lowest-level supervisory position, subsection head *(kakaricho)* [6].

Given the system of age-graded internal promotion, the figures suggest that it will be a very long time before women are well represented in corporate management. A major mechanism for blocking women from the promotion ladder is to exclude them from transfers to branch officer or posts far away from their homes, which means they are unable to acquire the range of experience needed for promotion to a managerial position. About two-thirds of the firms surveyed currently do this, and most intend to continue the practice despite the new law [6].

In 1979, as part of the background research for the new law, a Cabinet-level commission surveyed all companies listed on the stock exchange and special corporations in the three major urban centres of Tokyo, Osaka, and Nagoya that were capitalized at over ¥500 million [8]. The 1,497 companies surveyed had an average work force of 3,321 and an average of 242 person in decision-making positions.

The study found that women constituted about a quarter (23.3%) of the work force in these large companies, but only 0.3 per cent of those in decision-making positions. Nine-tenths (89.5%) of the companies had no women at all in decision-making positions, and most of the remainder (7.8%) had only one or two women in such positions. Fewer than one per cent (0.7%) of the companies had 10 or more women in decision-making posts [8].

In the entire sample of 1,497 companies, employing almost five million people, the study was able to identify fewer than a thousand women in managerial positions. Two-thirds of the 996 women managers found by the study (66.5%) were at the section-head *(kachô)* level. Seven per cent were department heads *(bucho)*, and only 1.6 per cent were corporate officers [8].

In a companion study conducted in 1981, the same Cabinet-level commission surveyed women in decision-making positions in associations, organizations, unions, and co-operatives, institutions that fell outside the purview of the earlier study. Eighty-five per cent of these institutions had no women in decision-making positions, and only five per cent had more than one woman [9]. Women make up 40.1 per cent of the work force, but only 0.5 per cent of management in these organizations, an even greater disparity than in corporation listed on the stock exchange. [9].

The Public Sector

The situation of women in the public sector is similar. Local, prefectural, and national levels of government all hire permanent white-collar employees directly out of school. Like private corporations, they hire both men and women, but expect to retain the men until retirement in their mid-fifties and to lose many of the women within a few years. However, government is not quite as free as the private sector to discriminate against women, because the laws governing the hiring and promotion of public employees provide some protection. Women schoolteachers, for example, routinely work until the mandatory retirement age, even if they marry and have children. Many are promoted to grade-level or discipline supervisor, and some achieve the rank of principal.

Even in the regular administrative areas of the public sector, it is now difficult for government not to hire women for permanent positions if they have competitive qualifications. Once hired, they have at least a claim to equal treatment, but they may not receive it. Although the numbers are still small, there are women in managerial positions at all three levels of government. In the national government, only 0.7 per cent of managers at the *kacho* level, and 0.8 per cent at the *bucho* level, are women. At the prefectural level the numbers are about the same. These numbers reflect the government's resistance to hiring women in the upper career tracks in earlier years.

Although one still needs a magnifying glass to read these numbers, 0.8 per cent women managers in government is more than twice the 0.3 per cent women managers in large corporations. Observing that there may be somewhat more opportunity in the public sector, some highly talented and ambitious young women have begun directing their aspirations toward government, where the door is slightly ajar, rather than toward private industry, where it remains essentially closed.

Enterprise Scale in the Japanese Economy

It is clear that women managers are rare in the corporate world, and barely more visible in government. To stop at this point, however, would seriously distort the actual situation of women managers in Japan. In fact, there are women in managerial positions just about everywhere in Japan except in the largest corporations. To get a proper perspective on the situation, the overall pattern of firm size in Japan must be examined in more detail.

In general, Japanese firms are much smaller than their American counterparts. Instead of having one giant corporation under central control with a proliferation of divisions, the Japanese tend to have smaller separate companies interlocked into tight vertical networks. The overall group of companies may be as large as a giant American conglomerate, but it is actually made up of many, sometimes several hundred, separate companies, ranging in size from large corporations listed on the stock exchange down to tiny firms employing fewer than five people. In manufacturing, the firms are linked through subcontracting relationship; in service and merchandising, they are linked in distribution networks.

The definition of a large company varies by industry: 300 employees and capitalization at ¥ 100 million in manufacturing; 100 or more employees and capitalization at ¥ 30 million in wholesale firms; and 50 employees and capitalization at ¥ 10 million in retail enterprises. Even with these rather generous definitions, only 0.6 per cent of all Japanese corporations meet the definition of a large company. The overwhelming majority of firms (99.4%) are small or of medium size, and together they employ 81.1 per cent of all private-sector employees in the Japanese labour force. Three-quarters of all working women are employed in small or medium-size enterprises. Moreover, most of the growth in female labour-force participation in recent years has been in this area [10].

Thus, it is not surprising that women in managerial positions are most often found in small and medium-size enterprises. Nearly two and a half million Japanese women run their own (non-agricultural) businesses, most of which have fewer than five employees [1]. Yet, in 1984, there were 25,447 women serving as presidents of companies with five or more employees, a 10.5 per cent increase over the previous year [11]. Although the measures are not exactly comparable, they do suggest that the smaller the firm, the more likely it is to be run by a woman.

In a 1983 study of 37 small retail businesses in a single commercial neighbourhood, Steinhoff[2] found women heavily involved in running nearly all of the shops, but in varying capacities. Some shops were owned and run by women whose husbands worked as salaried men. A few women had inherited a business, including one daughter-in-law who had been brought into the family to take over her mother-in-law's shop. The majority were family businesses run jointly by husband and wife, often with each spouse running a branch store in a different location. In the few businesses large enough to have non-family employees, the wife was the major supervisor and decision maker in daily operations.

Komatsu [11] sees three factors behind the rapid increase in women company presidents. The first is the general changes—*e.g.*, smaller family size, reduced household work, and women's recognition that they can do what used to be defined as men's work—that are pushing women out of the home and into more external activities. Second, the structural problems involved in penetrating the existing corporate system force women to act on their own. Third, leisure and volunteer activities are giving rise to new types of enterprises that women can develop.

A 1986 popular magazine article lists the ten most common types of enterprises run by a women president. At the top of the list are companies that retail women's or children's clothing

(1,591). Real estate agencies (803) are second, followed by retail kimono and bedding stores (749). Fourth on the list are inns and hotels (710); construction (694) outranks restaurants (639) and bars and cabarets (639). The remaining three types in the top ten are retail fuel companies (495), general retail stores (415), and barber and beauty shops (400). The 1985 annual income of the top 200 companies with women presidents ranged from a photo typesetting machine company, with earnings of $25 million, down to a petrochemical company earning under $1 million, in 1985 dollars [11]. These figures for the top 200 companies suggest that the overwhelming majority of companies headed by women are quite small.

Background and Characteristics of Women Managers

The Prime Minister's Office studies of women in decision-making positions in large corporations provide the most reliable data on the most invisible category of women managers. The educational levels of women managers were surprisingly low for contemporary Japan: about one-third had only middle-school education, and another third, high-school education. Only 16.6 per cent had four-year college degrees, and fewer than one per cent had a graduate degree. Their average age was 49.8 years, yet about two-thirds of the women in decision-making positions were unmarried. They had worked for the same company for an average of 28.6 years [8].

It is clear from these findings that the women who did attain managerial positions in large corporations did not do so through the white-collar-employee route that is now the norm for such companies. These women managers may be located in traditionally female occupations such as nursing or working as telephone operators or in businesses connected with women's apparel, from which it is possible to rise to mid-level supervisory positions. Another possibility is that some large companies in domestic product areas may have grown from small and medium-sized enterprises during the past three decades, promoting some long-term female employees in the process.

A second conclusion that may be drawn from these findings is that women who have achieved managerial rank in large corporations have done so after long service to the company, largely at the expense of marriage and motherhood. This is consistent with the inference that women in management may be located primarily in traditionally female occupations. In contrast to the usual pattern of female employment in large companies, such occupations provide an alternative to the long-term economic security of marriage, and eventually reward the competent and experienced unmarried employee with some opportunity for promotion. The general absence of married women with children among the ranks of corporate management also attests to the management culture barriers discussed earlier.

Takagi and Nakamura [12] conducted a questionnaire study, for the Japanese Association of Women Executives (JAWE), that included 66 women in positions ranging from section chief to corporate officer. Over half the women in the study were from corporations having more than a thousand employees. Two-thirds were college graduates, and another 13 per cent were junior-college graduates. The average age of the managers was 45. Slightly over one-half of the women in the JAWE study were married, and the great majority of those (86%) had children. Three-fourths reported that their husbands were quite co-operative about their work [12].

These results differ considerably from the Prime Minister's Office survey. The JAWE study sample included relatively more women with high managerial rank, and their mean age was younger; but it also included managers in smaller companies. The differences may be an artifact of the sample, or they may reflect future trends.

Several other recent studies of women managers in small and medium-size companies report results similar to the JAWE study [10, 11, 13]. The picture that emerges from these various studies is that women managers are generally not highly educated, although college training seems increasingly to be the norm. Among women who work their way up from employee to managerial status, those with appropriate professional qualifications can be promoted to central managerial posts, but women without qualifications rarely rise higher than chief of a secretarial or accounting section.

Women managers in small and medium-size enterprises are more likely to be married and have children, although the possibility of combined roles may be increasing in larger firms as well. Women in management appear to come from families that encourage women to work and study. A substantial minority have working mothers as role models. Their fathers tend to be in professional or managerial occupations that offer role models for their daughters, and also possibly the capital to help realize their ambitions.

Career Paths of Women Managers

Using life history interviewing methods, Nohata [14] found a variety of career patterns among Japanese women managers. This supports the view that women achieve managerial positions by working around the dominant male career pattern, rather than competing within it. American studies have also found that women often take routes different from those of men to achieve the same managerial positions.

The JAWE study did not trace career paths directly, but the survey results provide some indication of women managers' experiences and attitudes. Although only about half reported that becoming a manager had been an important goal for them, the overwhelming majority (87%) found it advantageous to be one. About a third of them had decided while they were still students that they would continue working. Another 16.7 per cent decided after they began to work, but 28.8 per cent decided only after they had discovered how interesting the work was. Over ninety per cent had decided to continue working before they married or had a child [12]. These findings suggest that the women achieved managerial status because of special ability and circumstance, unlike Japanese men, who are directed toward such careers from childhood.

The women managers believed firmly that there was no difference in ability between male and female managers, but that women were at a disadvantage in the world of business. They agreed overwhelmingly that being able to handle male-female issues in business cleverly was an essential skill for women managers. Over two-thirds reported that there were many people available to help them in their careers, suggesting that these women had been able to acquire a network of patrons and allies just as male managers do [12].

Almost half of the women managers had changed jobs at some point in the past. Furthermore, only half said they were willing to transfer to a different office if their job required it [12]. Their unwillingness to make internal transfers coincides with the general policy of large companies not to transfer women, but the record suggests these women may have resolved the problem in the past by changing jobs. Such flexibility about leaving an employer works to women's disadvantage in the largest companies, but may open up opportunities for them in smaller firms that can use their experience.

If effective career strategies for women within larger corporations remain murky, the picture is somewhat clearer and easier to evaluate for women who are actually running or heading smaller firms. The heads of Japanese companies are customarily divided into three types: founders, relatives of founders, or employees who have worked their way up. This categorization reflects the traditional family-enterprise orientation of Japanese society. Founders are generally characterized as dynamic and aggressive entrepreneurs who maintain firm personal control over the enterprise; successors tend to rely more heavily on staff; employees who work their way up tend to have a more bureaucratic, team-oriented, managerial style.

A Keio research group found that each of these three categories required further specification in order to reflect the actual career paths of women who inherited family businesses or began their own with prior managerial experience ranging from zero to years of full partnership. Older women were more likely to have been thrust into a managerial role by circumstances, whereas younger women were more likely to have achieved it by the accumulation of relevant experiences. The study also found that women managers placed more value on realization of their ideals and self-actualization than on social and monetary success. They were therefore more likely to maintain their enterprise at an appropriate size with a good rate of profit rather than risk expansion [10].

Women managers were not necessarily supportive of increased opportunity for other women. Many women managers in their late fifties or older did not treat female employees as they treated male employees, and they often imposed the same constraints on female employees as the large corporations do. Regardless of age, women managers made heavy use of middle-aged, part-time, female workers [10].

Most women founders in the Esso-sponsored study by Komatsu [11] said they would appoint women to managerial posts the same as men, and would consider appointing a women to succeed them. Successors, on the other hand, said they would consider appointing women only to certain areas of work. Attitudes toward managerial posts for women also varied sharply by industry, support for women's advancement being more common among presidents of service and retail businesses, and more negative attitudes toward women prevailing in manufacturing. Opinion was also sharply divided by age, younger women presidents favouring managerial opportunities for women, and women over 55 being sharply opposed [15].

Although the distinction in attitudes between founders and successors could be interpreted as an indication that attitudes toward women in management become more discriminatory as a company matures, generational differences must be taken into account, since in both studies women successors tended to be older than women founders. Women under fifty who were educated in the postwar era have fundamentally different attitudes toward women's achievement, which are less likely to change as they grow older, or as the companies they manage mature. It seems highly unlikely that the next generation of women successors will be as conservative as the present one.

Prospects for the Future

There is some indication that large companies are beginning to offer more promotion opportunities to women. In a recent study, primarily of companies listed on the stock exchange, 64 per cent said they would promote women college graduates if they had the same abilities as men. The larger the company, the greater the professed support for promotion of qualified women. When asked what they thought of the current trend for women to work for a longer period of time, 84 per cent of the companies said it was acceptable if the women was strongly motivated; but only six per cent of the companies found the trend desirable [16]. The distinction implied here between broad support for the unusually motivated career women and continuing resistance to offering career opportunities to all women is reflected in a recent proposal by a committee of the Kanto Managers Association. Charged with formulating a response to the new Equal Opportunity Law, the committee suggested that companies create a two-track system that would offer promotion opportunities to highly qualified and motivated women, but leave intact the present system of high turnover positions for most women. The committee said it was not economically feasible for companies to offer management training opportunities to all women employees.[3]

Overall, the studies reviewed here suggest that opportunities for women in management are likely to increase in the future, but not as rapidly in the large corporations, from which women are currently most sharply excluded. For a very limited number of unusually qualified women, opportunities may expand; but women who seek careers in large bureaucracies probably will continue to find somewhat more opportunity for advancement in the public sector.[4]

Small and medium-size enterprises, in which three-quarters of all women are employed, represent a dynamic growth area for women with managerial ambitions. Because there is greater job mobility in these smaller-scale enterprises, there may be considerable movement into such firms by women with previous experience in large corporations. This would include both women who leave to start their own firms and women who are hired by existing firms because of their skills and experience.

As more educated women with work experience either remain in the labour force through the childbearing years or return after only a few years' absence, cultural images of the working married women are likely to change, as they have elsewhere. The middle-class status symbol of a nonworking wife, a relatively recent, postwar addition to Japanese culture, already shows signs of decline.

The proportion of new women employees who seek promotion has more than doubled in the past two years, from 12.5 per cent in 1984 to 28.4 per cent in 1986.[5] In the same two years, there have appeared two new magazines aimed at Japanese career-oriented women. Whether such women will find an environment in which to realize their desires is problematic, as sex roles are now in transition in Japan.

The owners of small family businesses in Japan now encourage their sons to get a higher education and to move into the more prestigious world of the white collar "salaryman." Fewer expect that their children will take over the family firm, with its traditional pattern of participation by the wife. The same families also envision their daughters as the nonworking wives of salaried employees. Thus, the middle-class pattern of the white-collar "salaryman" with his nonworking wife remains a cultural ideal of upward mobility for the children of small-business families, although most will not make it into the large corporations.

At the same time, there is increasing evidence that nonworking, middle-class housewives married to "salarymen" now encourage their daughters to prepare for careers outside the home. It is not at all clear, however, that the same mothers are rearing their sons to accommodate a wife with a career. To the extent that the Japanese corporate world continues to freeze women out of managerial positions and to expect that a male manager will have a nonworking wife as a personal support system, these differing parental encouragements point toward both domestic and workplace conflict in the future.

Much of this potential for conflict is likely to be defused, however, by the dynamism and fluidity of the small and medium-size enterprise sector. Despite long-standing predictions, this sector does not seem to be decreasing in size or significance in the Japanese economy. Moreover, despite the elitism of the Japanese education system and large corporations, a great deal of talent still flows into small and medium-size enterprises. If that is the sector that accommodates women's growing career aspirations, still more talent will find its way there.

In sum, the future appears to offer increasing opportunities for women in management in Japan, but there will still be some glaring blank spots. Ambitious young Japanese women will have to seek out opportunities for advancement shrewdly, and pick their mates carefully.

NOTES

1. Kazuko Tanaka (1976) "Female Labour Force Participation in Japan." Unpublished paper, University of Hawaii.
2. P.G. Steinhoff (1983) Unpublished data.
3. Kanto Managers Association (1986) "Danjo Koyo Kikai Kinto Ho to Kore Kara no Koyo Kanri no Hoko" [The Equal Employment Opportunity Law and the Future Direction of Employee Management]. Tokyo: Kanto Managers Association.
4. For Japanese women with good foreign-language skills, there may be more opportunity for advancement in foreign companies. No data on this are available, however, and this sector remains a very small part of the overall employment picture.
5. Taiyo Kobe Bank Management Consulting Office (1986) "Mo Sugu Shakaijin: Shinnyu Shain no Ishiki Chosa" [Soon They'll Be Full Members of Society: Attitude Survey of New Employees]. Kobe: Taiyo Kobe Bank Management Consulting Office.

REFERENCES

1. Women's Bureau (1986) *Fujin Rodo no Jitsujo* [The Actual Condition of Women Workers, 1986]. Tokyo: Printing Office, Ministry of Finance.
2. Saxonhouse, G. (1976) "Country Girls and Communication among Competitors in the Japanese Cotton-spinning Industry." In H. Patrick (Ed.), *Japanese Industrialization and Its Social Consequences.* Berkeley, CA: University of California Press.
3. Coleman, S. (1983), *Family Planning in Japanese Society: Traditional Birth Control in a Modern Urban Culture.* Princeton, NJ: Princeton University Press.
4. Vogel, E. (1968), *Japan's New Middle Class.* Berkeley, CA: University of California Press.
5. Sugawara, M. (1985) "Josei Kanrishoku no Hikari to Kage" [Light and Shadows of Women Managers]. In H. Hara and A. Sugiyama (Eds.), *Hataraku Onnatachi no Jidai* [Working Women's Era]. Tokyo: Nihon Hososhuppankyokai.

6. Labour Administration Research Institute (1986) *Danjo Koyo Kikai Kinto Ho ni Taisuru Kigyo on Taio Jokyo o Miru* [A Look at How Enterprises Have Responded to the Equal Employment Opportunity Law]. Tokyo: Labour Administration Research Institute.

7. Women's Bureau (1984) *Joshi Rodosha no Koyokanri ni Kansuru Chosa* [Research on Employment Management of Women Workers]. Tokyo: Women's Bureau.

8. Prime Minister's Office, Women's Section (1979) *Fujin no Hoshinketteisanka jokyochosa Hokokusho* [Report of Research on the Conditions of Women's Participation in Decision Making]. Tokyo: Prime Minister's Office.

9. Prime Minister's Office, Women's Section (1981) *Fujin no Hoshinket-teisanka jokyochosa Hokokusho (Kaisha igai no hojin, hojin de nai dantai)* [Report of Research on the Condition of Women's Participation in Decision Making (Corporations Other than Companies, and Unincorporated Associations)]. Tokyo: Prime Minister's Office.

10. Iwao, S., Hara, H., and Muramatsu, Y. (1982) "Chushokigyo ni okeru Josei Keiesha no Seichoreki Seikatsu Keieikan—Tonia 42 sha (42 mei) no Mensetsuchôsa ni motozuku Jireikenkyu" [The career, Living Conditions, and Management Attitudes of Women Managers in Small and Medium-sized Enterprises— Research Based on Interviews with 42 Companies (42 Persons) in Tokyo]. *Soshiki kodo kenkyu, 9,* 1-120.

11. Komatsu, M. (1986) "Joseishacho wa Kigyo Shakai wo kô kaeru" [Women presidents—How They Are Changing Industry and Soceity]. *Shukan Diamond,* 11 February, pp. 82-87.

12. Takagi, H., and Nakamura, N. (1986) *Joseikanrishoku no Yaruki to Noryoku soshite Shinshutsu* [Women Managers' Desires, Talent, and Advancement]. Tokyo: Japanese Association of Women Executives.

13. Hirano, T. (1981) "Josei no Shokugyo Keisei to Kankyo" [The Structure and Circumstances of Women's Work]. *Musashino Joshidaigaku Kiyo, 16,* 59-74.

14. Nohata, M. (1986) "Joseiyakushokusha no Career Keiseikatei to Sokushinshoyoin." [Factors and Process of Career Formation of Managerial Women]. *Shakaigaku Hyoron, 34,* 438-56.

15. Komatsu, M. (1984) "Joseikeieisha no Ningenzo—Sogyosha no Seishindojo wo Saguru" [A Human Picture of Women Managers Searching for the Spirit of Founders]. *Josei no tame no Esso Kenkyu Shoreiseido Kenkyuhokokushu Esso Sekiyu Kabushikigaisha, 3,* 3-4.

16. Japan Manpower Administration Research Institute (1986) *Shorai Arubeki Jinji Kanri wo Kangaeru tame no Kiso Chosa 1985,* [1985 Research for Consideration of Desirable Manpower Mangement in the Future]. Tokyo: Japan Manpower Administration Research Institute.

12

Education and Attainment A Study of Women of Dalit Groups

Historical Background

The history of the movement for improving women's status all over the world and especially in India shows emphasis from the beginning on education as the most significant instrument for changing women's subjugated position in society. Increase of educational facilities and opportunities and the removal of traditional barriers on entry of women to particular branches and levels of education, came to be supported by champions of women's emancipation from the 19th Century onwards. Social reformers in India emphasized the crucial importance of education of women to improve their status in society. According to the reformers, the main purpose for educating women was not to make them more efficient and active units in the process of socio-economic or political development, but to make them more capable of fulfilling their traditional roles in society as wives and mothers. Education for women was regarded as a means to improve their status within the family, and not to equip them to play any economic role in the wider social context. According to R.C. Majumdar, the absence of any economic compulsion was in fact, the main reason for the slow progress of women's education in this country. Because of their reluctance to interfere in social matters, the colonial authorities generally supported the purely humanitarian and a limited view of women's education. Only when the problem of reaching education and health services to the women of the country arose, did the authorities take cognizance of the fact that there was need for women teachers and doctors. Since this was not possible without training women in these professions, the importances of these two vocations outside the familial roles had to be incorporated in the programmes for women's education. The post-Independence era saw a new dimension added to women's education. The constitution had accepted equality of women and their need to play multiple roles in society. "It was for the first time accepted that the general purpose and objective of women's education was in no way different from the purpose and objective of men's education. It was decided that at the secondary and even at the university stage women's education should have a vocational/occupational bias. In the progressive society of tomorrow, life should be a joint venture for men and women. Men should share the responsibility of parenthood and home making with women and women in their turn should share the social and economic responsibilities of men."*

The emphasis on education equipping women to carry out their multiple roles as citizens, housewives, mothers, contributors to the family income and builders of the new society helped as choice ingredient for the improvement of their status.

The National Committee on Women's Education had reviewed the progress of women's education before, during and after Independence and concluded that inspite of the direct action taken by the states for this purpose after Independence, "the education of women has not made satisfactory progress between 1947-57." But one must comment on the change of situation in later years. For women's education as social institution has

---

* Report of the Committee on Differentiation of Curricula for boys and girls, Government of India, 1954, Chapter IV.

developed certain convictions for the society. Anderson and Parker mention some important educational convictions of the American Society and they are applicable to Indian society as it is developing on the American model to an extent.

Among these convictions the first is:

(i) Education can solve problems. The underlying conviction in America is that education is a cure—all that can solve most of the social problems of our society and lead the way to human betterment.

(ii) Education for all: The second conviction is that every one should be educated.

(iii) Equal opportunity for all. A third conviction which has been a symbol of our democratic society, is that opportunity to obtain education should be equal to all. (Anderson and Parker, 1964. In spite of this education for women has lagged behind.

Even during the phase where education spread in India the untouchables remained backward. The progress of education in this community was very slow. They lacked in resources to cope with education. It took a long time for society to change their views regarding educating scheduled caste men, hence the question of education of scheduled caste women could not be thought of during this period. Due to the male dominated culture and other various reasons mentioned above scheduled caste women entered the field of education very late. Due to low status and ill paying traditional occupations the scheduled caste expected their children to work on daily wages in their early years instead of studying in school. This attitude made the nature of difficulties two fold for those who are trying to educate themselves. First lack of inspiration, guidance from family members and momentary help and second humiliating treatment and opposition from higher caste Hindus added to the troubles of scheduled caste women. As a result the percentage of untouchable or scheduled caste women was very low in schools and colleges. Mahatma Gandhi advocated the removal of untouchability, however, the specific plan regarding the education of scheduled caste men and women was very low in schools and colleges.

The education of scheduled caste men and women was thus over shadowed by the political upheaval. Thus politics took a precedence over social reform or the thought of total change in the social structure.

After independence the new constitution of free-India made untouchability—unlawful, thus providing complete security to the Scheduled Caste section of Indian society. But in reality the practice of untouchability persisted in many subtle ways. As a result (1) the given opportunities were not utilized fully (2) those who were trying to utilize the opportunities were opposed by their own caste people and by other higher castes. This resulted in conflicts, problems and tensions.

Transition from Education for the Sake of Learning to Education for Employment

The traditional social structure of Indian society which perpetuated social inequality among the castes and between the sexes received a big jolt with the emergence of the British Rule in India. The British rule brought into the Indian society a new industrial technology, Christianity and the System of Universal secular liberal education. These changes shook the very foundation of the traditional social structure, namely belief in Dharma, Karma and Punarjanma.

As compared with other high castes, the concept of education was introduced to the scheduled caste rather late. But social, economic constraints often compell the scheduled caste individual to take up any available job. Very few individuals from the untouchable community possess his own or ancestral property. Nor can they raise capital for starting a business as they have practically no security to pledge to secure a loan. Naturally an individual of a scheduled caste opts for a permanent employment with the help of educational qualifications. "First he wants to raise his economic status and standard of living of his family and secondly by securing higher status, he wants to get recognition by other higher castes for him and his family. Member of scheduled caste think that education will raise their level of thoughts; will change attitude towards life and on account of this progressive change they will be able to change the attitude of wider society towards their group. Every educated untouchable and each of them undergoing education entertains at his heart these notions'. (Tribhuvan, 1977). One of the aims of education is to create skills and occupational efficiency which in turn, makes the individual self-sufficient and helps to raise the economic standard and social status of the person. This becomes a means of social change. Brembeck says, "all classes use education as an agent of social change, they do not use it in the same way, *e.g.*, the middle classes are good consumers of education and constantly demand more for their children. The working class is a selective consumer of education. But when any family of middle, working or lower class sends its children to school, it usually has some social goals in mind and achieving that goal through education involves some social change, great or small. For lower classes change is more drastic (Brembeck Cole, S., 1966).

Social Mobility and Education

The minimization of the difference in the level of literacy among the lower class and upper class helps to reduce the social distance and social differences. With higher education an individual becomes more capable and can achieve membership in higher class. The interaction between education and social stratification directly influences social mobility. Social mobility is the only way in which the scheduled caste could be brought into the mainstream.

I

To find out the utilizations of educational opportunities given to the Scheduled Castes in Maharashtra we shall review some of the available data on retention and drop out of Scheduled Castes students.

Broadly speaking, two factors bio-genic and socio-genic obstruct or prevent the total development of a child. Bio-genic or inherent are transmitted through parental genes, put a limit to the child's growth and development. "He has to suffer the inherited biological disadvantages and inadequacies." The socio-genic factors are outside this child in the socio-economic conditions availed to an individual. This factor may have the impact of deprivation upon various dimensions of psychological and educational development of the child. Keeping these important factors in mind a constant effort has been made of imparting scholastic education to the scheduled caste, scheduled tribe and other minority groups. Many of our educational policies, financial and other aids, have been granted to help these children, yet the outcome does not seem to be as positive as one would desire. Chitnis's Statistics shows that despite such attempts, the percentage of irregular school attendance and school dropouts is higher in the case of scheduled caste children. One can assert that those who drop out from school lack cognitive skills, which assist the child to go through his scholastic education. Staying out from school or class is not a problem: It is a symptom of a problem which is less evident. In view of the negative experiences which a scheduled caste child encounters in school, staying out of school may be the only option available. It is presumed that once the school climate is perceived supportive by a scheduled caste child it would lead him to attend his school regularly and maintain the required motivation for learning. "Ideally a school should present such a climate in which meaningful learning experiences are possible. The role of school climate becomes even more salient when our concern is the education of disadvantaged children, particularly belonging to the scheduled caste." (Panda Namimta, 1980). Intutively, it appears that a majority school presents a climate which is less supportive for minority group children where they experience a less of ethnic identity. scheduled caste and scheduled tribe students in majority schools showed low need for achievement, poor academic self-concept, high fear of failure and unrealistic aspirations as compared to scheduled caste and scheduled tribes students in minority schools.

Social Commitment by the Constitution

The constitution places a special responsibility on the Government for the educational advancement of the scheduled castes and scheduled tribes. A high priority was, therefore, given to the implementation of schemes for educational advancement of these communities, during all the five year plans so far.

The rigid caste system totally debarred the scheduled castes and scheduled tribes from education in the olden days. As a result they were mostly illiterate and did not recognise the importance of education for gaining economic and social mobility. The Centre and State Governments invested heavily on the education of the scheduled castes and scheduled tribes, because the moulders of Independent India felt that education is an effective mechanism for achieving upward mobility in modern society. Equality of educational opportunities thus became one of the cherished goals of the government.

The leaders of the freedom movement and the framers of the Constitution of India were fully alive to the necessity of the improvement of their lot. The Constitution, therefore, incorporates a number of provisions for the purpose. The State is prohibited from discriminating against any citizen on the basis of caste [Art. 15 (1)]; there shall be no discrimination in public employment on the basis of caste [Art. 16 (4)] access to public places (like wells, shops, restaurants etc. has been made open to all [Art. 15 (2)]; untouchability has been abolished (Art. 17) and has also been made punishable by law; Hindu temples have been made open to all Hindus [Art. 15 (2) (5)]; admissible to State-run and State-aided educational institutions has been made open to all [Art. 29 (2)]. Above all, protective discrimination by the State in their favour generally has been provided under Art. 15 (4), and in government jobs under Article 16 (4). The Directive principles imposes special obligation on the State to 'protect them from social injustice and all forms of exploitation'. One of the directive principle of State policy in the constitution enjoining that the State shall provide a job or occupation. After Independence, Indian Constitution guaranteed the right to education to all the Indian vocationals irrespective of their caste and creed.

Protective Discrimination

While the point that the situation of scheduled castes needs ameliorative action is hardly disputable, the crucial question that remains is whether they, as members of the former untouchable castes, are deserving of special protective discrimination any more than others who are economically or otherwise disadvantaged and do not belong to the scheduled castes. One of the major assumptions underlying the protective provisions and programmes for the scheduled castes seems to have been that persons belonging to these caste are distinctly more disadvantaged than others belonging to comparable socio-economic positions. It has also been assumed that the added disadvantage would accrue not only from a history of caste discrimination suffered by members of these castes but also from the possibility of continued practice of discrimination in subtle forms. Continuation of the protective discrimination accorded to the scheduled castes in justifiable only if all these assumptions continue to hold true, unless, of course, it is justified on the grounds of contribution and a moral obligation to atone for injustice meted out to the untouchables and other lower castes in the past. Further, Marc Galanter extended the concept of protective discrimination to compensatory discrimination which seems to be more justifiable in context to the scheduled castes. His thesis is based on the number of years of deprivations experienced by scheduled castes which should be compensated, so that they enter the mainstream.

"Preferences are of three basic types. First there are reservations which allot or facilitate access to valued positions or resources. The most important instances of this type are reserved seats in legislatures, reservation of posts in government services, and reservation of places in academic institutions (especially the coveted higher technical and professional colleges). To a lesser extent, the reservation device is also used in the distribution of land allotments, housing and other scarce resources. Second, there are programmes involving expenditure or provision of services—*e.g.*, scholarships, grants, loans, land allotments, health care, legal aid, to a beneficiary group beyond comparable expenditures for others. Third there are special protections. These distributive schemes are accompanied by efforts to protect the backward classes from being exploited and victimized." (Galanter, 1984).

Education of Scheduled Castes

The issue of imparting scholastic education to the scheduled castes and scheduled tribes and other minority groups consistently figures in most of our educational policies. Education, with a fervent hope that it widens the mind, trains the critical faculties of thought and judgment has always been valued highly by all societies and cultures. It is considered the sine qua non for the freedom from the shackles of ignorance, dependency, poverty etc. Through the successive Five Year Plans the Government and the Planning Commission sought to ameliorate the problems and tried to raise the socio-economic levels of the people in India. However, three decades of development has not had the desired effect on the socially, economically and educationally handicapped groups. (Sixth Five Year Plan, 1980-85).

Every nation hopes to achieve social progress through education, because education in the developing societies is expected not only to inspire varied skills but also to inculcate modern values. It is widely recognised that the spread of education formal or non-formal plays a vital role in the socio-economic and cultural modernization of the country. It is believed that higher literacy rate is an index of greater economic development and modernization in society. For the equalization of educational opportunities would pave the way for equalization of opportunities in all spheres of social life. Thus the destiny of India is now being shaped in her class room. By 1973-74 the student population had indeed a remarkable increase. Not only the number of primary schools risen to five lakhs, but the roll had increased to six crore 38 lakhs. The secondary schools were approximately a lakh in number and had one crore 50 lakhs pupils. The Universities did not fall far behind for there were more than a hundred universities with four thousand colleges affiliated to them. 34 lakhs students received higher education in these colleges. The expenditure on education had risen from 114 crores in 1950-51 to 1800 crores in 1973-74 and now in 1977 has reached the high mark of 2200 crores.

Yet the total number of literatures is not as expected. For they are not in keeping with the expenditure incurred over the years. The literacy percentage in India was 16.6 in 1951 and 29.3 per cent today.

It was also noticed that the scheduled castes and scheduled tribes fall short of the general literacy rate as can be seen from the Table 12.1. There is no doubt that literacy in all the above categories have increased. It is a salient point to note that in the figures of literates of the total population, scheduled castes and scheduled tribes are included.

Table 12.1

Percentage of Literates in Maharashtra

Population	*1961*	*1971*	*1981*
Total Population	29.82%	39.78%	58.78%
Scheduled Castes	15.79%	26.43%	40.13%
Scheduled Tribes	NA	11.74%	12.35%

N.A. = Not Available

Thus on analysis it is found that the literacy of population roughly work out to 4 : 2 : 1 for other communities, Scheduled Castes and Scheduled Tribes respectively.

Magnitude of Drop-outs in Maharashtra

When we scrutinize Table 12.2 and 12.3, they indicate the retention of students in school, from which we can see that there are school-drop-outs at every stage and they reveal a uniform pattern. There is a progressive increase in enrolment of students, but the heavy drop outs reduce this enhanced enrolement. In the final analysis the wastage as seen from these tables for girls is 89.1 and for boys it is 79.6 per cent.

The rate of those who left school from 1972 to 1982 remains static. That is amongst each group though there is a differential rate of drop-out, it is maintained constant without any check over the years.

The data clearly shows the persistence of drop-out of students in Maharashtra remains unabated. In a year's time after joinig schools as many as 42.4 per cent girls and 35.4 per cent of boys drop out of school. The colossal wastage of educational facilities is further witnessed in Standard V. Education wastage is much more in the primary stage than in the secondary stage. We can correlate this factor to single teacher schools and

Table 12.2

Statement Showing Rates of Retention of Scheduled Caste Students (Excluding Neo-Buddhists) in Maharashtra State (1972-73 to 1981-82): (GIRLS)

Year	*I*	*II*	*III*	*IV*	*V*	*VI*	*VII*	*VIII*	*IX*	*X*
1972-73	83296 (100.0)									
1973-74	86441 (100.0)	47944 (57.6)								
1974-75	97981 (100.0)	49345 (57.1)	34879 (41.9)							
1975-76	98656 (100.0)	52650 (53.7)	37124 (42.9)	26795 (32.2)						
1976-77	101440 (100.0)	50920 (51.6)	35780 (36.5)	24860 (28.8)	20650 (24.8)					
1977-78	109732 (100.0)	60083 (59.2)	41721 (42.3)	29367 (30.0)	24727 (28.6)	17716 (21.3)				
1978-79	115421 (100.0)	62434 (57.4)	44480 (43.8)	31107 (31.5)	25181 (25.7)	18754 (21.7)	14269 (17.1)			
1979-80	122613 (100.0)	68550 (59.4)	49188 (44.8)	35704 (35.2)	28087 (28.5)	21212 (21.6)	16480 (19.1)	12498 (15.0)		
1980-81	120283 (100.0)	76256 (62.2)	55077 (47.7)	39391 (35.9)	32150 (31.7)	24147 (24.5)	19185 (19.6)	14582 (16.9)	11491 (13.8)	
1981-82	122237 (100,0)	80164 (66.6)	60279 (49.2)	42886 (37.2)	34901 (31.8)	26994 (26.6)	20976 (21.3)	16681 (17.0)	12894 (14.9)	9097 (10.9)

(Figures for 1976-77 are estimated).

Table 12.3

Statement Showing Rates of Retention of Scheduled Caste Students (Excluding Neo-Buddhists) in Maharashtra State (1972-73 to 1981-82): (BOYS)

Year	I	II	III	IV	V	VI	VII	VIII	IX	X
1972-73	128957 (100.0)									
1973-74	132457 (100.0)	83326 (64.6)								
1974-75	14293 (100.0)	88549 (66.9)	69268 (53.7)							
1975-76	145184 (100.0)	90456 (63.5)	71092 (53.7)	55851 (37.5)						
1976-77	144080 (100.0)	87420 (60.2)	65560 (46.0)	51870 (39.2)	45740 (35.5)					
1977-78	150256 (100.0)	97572 (67.7)	70771 (48.7)	55581 (39.0)	50453 (38.1)	39245 (30.4)				
1978-79	154435 (100.0)	99353 (66.1)	77948 (54.1)	58492 (40.3)	51974 (36.5)	41885 (31.6)	34253 (26.6)			
1979-80	156352 (100.0)	105817 (67.6)	83790 (55.8)	65099 (45.2)	57333 (39.5)	46030 (32.3)	37725 (28.5)	34162 (26.5)		
1980-81	153841 (100.0)	111800 (71.5)	91596 (59.3)	71369 (47.5)	64854 (45.0)	50444 (34.7)	42147 (29.6)	37744 (28.5)	30754 (23.9)	
1981-82	152883 (100.0)	112925 (73.4)	96165 (61.5)	77984 (50.5)	68264 (45.4)	56972 (39.5)	46494 (32.0)	42052 (29.5)	34669 (26.2)	26279 (20.4)

(Figures for 1976-77 are estimated).

lesser expenditure allotted by Government for this important sector. "It is generally recognized that absentism stagnation cause wastage and are universal problems effecting all educational institutions through out India, particularly at the primary stage of education. We believed this is because the educational picture broadly reflected this socio-economic background of inequality." (Naik, 1977).

When we try to take into consideration the factor of watage:

"Wastage is generally understood to connote the premature withdrawal of a child from school, before completing the last grade of the stage of education in which he is studying." (Sapra 1967).

This assessment of the problem of drop-outs leads us to look into its manifestations.

Factors Responsible for Drop-outs

There are various reasons responsible for these drop-outs. The causes for school drop outs could be categorically said to be due to the following factors:

(i) Psychological, comprising:
- *(a)* Intelligence of the child
- *(b)* External constraints
- *(c)* Widening gap in knowledge

(ii) Socio-economic:
- *(a)* Sociological factors
- *(b)* Cultural factors
- *(c)* Economic factors

(iii) Educational:
- *(a)* School System (Internal constraints)

II

We have briefly enumerated the factors responsible for school drop outs among scheduled castes girls but we have refrained from detailed analysis of these factors, which would by itself form a separate paper. At the same time the tremendous wastage in education in primary and secondary school level shows the non-achievements of scheduled caste girls in spite of protective discrimination, reservation and economic incentives. This categorically proves that the compensative equality principle applied in the case of scheduled castes has totally failed. Since psychological, socio-economic and educational factors were not taken into consideration adequately while planning for the total transformation of scheduled caste women into educated adults. Pointing out lacunae will not change the situation or solve the problems. We are therefore, giving an example of the 'achievers among scheduled caste women' from our recent study. An assessment of girls who complete their education and enter into white collared occupations has been made. These women can be considered as pioneers and trend setters for future planning of education and employment of scheduled caste women.

We have observed that women's education is given the last priority. We have also established that scheduled caste women are doubly disadvantaged. These women even though their achievements in comparison to other women seem meagure, yet we consider them as scheduled caste women who have been achievers. In this case we did not include the factor of socialization as they must have had some sort of push from their family members for pursuing their education.

This study was made to find out the impact of the education on scheduled caste women. Certain factors availed to scheduled caste women would be put to test:

(i) utilization of facilities given to scheduled caste women,
(ii) the aim of taking education by scheduled caste women,
(iii) achievement in education,
(iv) reasons for not taking higher education.

The methodology adopted will first be discussed and a brief socio-economic profile of the respondents will precede the data presentation and discussion.

Methodology

Exclusive studies on scheduled caste women's employment are practically non-existent. The reservation policy has opened the gates of employment to scheduled caste men as well as women. But quite a few scheduled caste women are not aware of their rights and therefore, do not take advantage of the reservations and policies of protective discrimination.

The Universe

Four urban areas in Maharashtra *i.e.*, Bombay, Pune, Nagpur and Aurangabad were chosen to represent the urban areas. The approach was from "Apex to Bottom", *i.e.*, starting with Bombay, which is a cosmopolitan metropolitan developed city to Aurangabad. Aurangabad, no doubt, is an urban industrialized city but persists in maintaining its traditional rural nature. Besides that it is the headquarter of an underdeveloped area in Maharashtra. In other two areas, Nagpur and Pune are in the middle range of development.

The tools of inquiry were a questionnaire/schedule supported by an interview. The questionnaire schedule was administered to 1200 educated employed scheduled caste women in these four cities of Maharashtra with an even sample of 300 respondents from each area. The questionnaire is exhaustive which included all the parameters of achievement problems of scheduled caste educated women.

Sample

Central Government and State Government offices, universities, hospitals, colleges, schools, banks and other offices where more than five scheduled caste women were employed were co-opted in our inquiry. A list of scheduled caste women employees was obtained and the respondents permission sought before the questionnaire was canvassed. A stratified random sampling method was adopted in data collection.

Life Style of Respondents

The socio-economic profile of the respondents indicates that a majority of the scheduled caste women are born in the cities, specially the group from Pune and Nagpur. A large number continue to be Hindus and only a few are Neo-Buddhists and infinitesimally small number are Christians. Mahars form the single largest group followed by the Chambhar caste, Mongs and Bhangis. Age-wise a majority of respondent belong to a young group as the cross section of respondents are 26 to 45 years of age. Place of birth order in a majority of castes indicates that a greater number of respondents are first born. The bulk of respondents have one or two sisters. Yet we find that most of the respondents come from large families. The single largest group of respondents belongs to married women, who have been married for six to ten years or one to five years. Most marriages have been within the sub-caste with only a few exceptions. Marriages in greater numbers have been arranged with consent from respondent and the unmarried women also would prefer to self choice marriage. Equal numbers are for and against divorce. Though respondents belonged to large families they themselves opted for small families. Greater number of respondents have illiterate parents and parents-in-law.

There are only one or two earning members besides the respondent. Respondents' fathers in greater numbers were class IV and III employees, labourers, small farmers or pensioners. Only a few had fathers who were officers, lecturer, headmaster or postmaster. Mothers of the respondents were mostly housewives those who worked were class IV and III employees. A similar trend was seen among the fathers-in-law and mothers-in-law of the respondents. Though a greater number of respondents' husbands were class III employees and a few were officers, at least 12 per cent of the respondents' brothers were professionals or officers. A majority claim to have a pooled income of the family between Rs. 1,000/- and Rs. 3,000/- per month.

Employment of scheduled caste women in white collar jobs was unheard of in the earlier generation. Women's earnings have a positive effect in savings resulting in nearly 40 per cent of the respondents possessing their own homes. Segregation of the scheduled caste is a thing of the past, now a majority live in a locality which has a mixed caste composition.

The socio-economic data forcefully enlightens us regarding the present situation of scheduled caste employed women. These women are from lower socio-economic strata, still had 'enlightened' parents who realized the importance of education for women. They also aspired for their daughters to achieve white collared employment, which would not only improve the economic status of the family, but also remove them from the performance of menial jobs. They therefore, socialized their daughters to the culture of functional education when they realized the facilities provided by government in education and employment. The parents of our respondents realized that the compensating discriminative policies ensured a job when minimum educational qualifications were achieved by girls. So they educated daughters to become secondary bread-winners in the natal or family of procreation.

Respondents and Education

We shall now turn our attention to the collected data regarding scheduled caste women in white collar jobs. These women do not belong to drop-out for they have reached upto the secondary school certificate level, passed the examination and managed to get jobs. The parental objectives in educating their daughters are seen in Table 12.4. The three main reasons as seen from the Table were:

(i) To get knowledge,
(ii) To raise income earning capacity,
(iii) For personal development.

Other reasons were:

(iv) To get a white collar job, and
(v) To get a better husband.

This means that the parents of respondents who were illiterate had tried to overcome their handicaps though education of their daughters.

Table 12.5 indicates the respondents' perception of taking education. Respondents sought education because:

(i) they wanted employment,
(ii) they wanted higher status in society,
(iii) education was their goal of life or an ambition,
(vi) it provides economic security,

Other reasons giving by the respondents were:

(v) for improving the standard of the family,
(vi) for self-satisfaction.

Table 12.4

Parental Objective in Educating the Respondents

Parent's objective in educating	*Bombay*	*Pune*	*Nagpur*	*Aurangabad*
To get knowledge	66 (22.00)	51 (17.00)	69 (23.00)	46 (15.33)
To get a white collared job	41 (13.66)	110 (36.66)	62 (20.66)	112 (37.33)
To get non-traditional job	17 (5.66)	8 (2.66)	15 (5.00)	30 (10.00)
To raise income earning capacity	69 (23.00)	23 (7.66)	37 (12.33)	79 (26.33)
For personal Development	67 (22.33)	88 (29.34)	92 (30.66)	29 (9.66)
To get a better husband	25 (8.34)	9 (3.00)	18 (6.00)	—
1 + 5 above or any other combination with 1 above	7 (2.33)	10 (3.33)	6 (2.00)	2 (0.66)
4 + 5 above	7 (2.33)	—	1 (0.33)	2 (0.66)
No Reply	1 (0.33)	1 (0.33)		
Total	300 (99.99)	300 (99.98)	300 (99.98)	300 (99.97)

The emphasis is more or less as we see is on security and better status (through job). This is understandable as the scheduled caste over the years have lacked them. The opportunity availed to them is taken seriously by women and they hope to make a better life for themselves.

The bulk of them have got a second class at the school final exams, which indicates that, had there been no reservations, these mediocare students would not have been eligible for a job. We must hasten to add that performance of these women is a reflection of the culture of education in their families, which shows a preponderance of negative attitude.

Table 12.5

Respondent's Reasons for Taking Higher Education

Reasons for taking Higher education	*Bombay*	*Pune*	*Nagpur*	*Aurangabad*
For employment	89 (29.67)	93 (31.00)	106 (35.33)	105 (35.00)
For economic security	45 (15.00)	30 (10.00)	29 (9.66)	42 (14.00)
For getting higher status in society	52 (17.33)	54 (18.00)	46 (15.33)	48 (16.00)
Education is a goal of life	49 (16.33)	47 (15.66)	52 (18.33)	61 (20.33)
For improving the standard of the family	28 (9.33)	43 (14.33)	34 (11.33)	25 (8.34)
Education is an asset to marriage	6 (2.00)	11 (3.67)	11 (3.67)	2 (0.66)
For Self satisfaction	26 (8.67)	21 (7.00)	21 (7.00)	16 (5.33)
Other combinations 1 + 2 + 3	2 (0.66)	—	—	1 (0.33)
Not taken higher education	3 (1.00)	1 (0.33)	1 (0.33)	—
Total	300 (99.99)	300 (99.99)	300 (99.98)	300 (99.99)

Amar Kumar Singh categorically mentioned that poverty and prejudice prevent the development and growth of the potentialities of the individual. Poverty has direct and visible impact on the child, while the adverse effect of the prejudice is somewhat more subtle, indirect and invisible than that of poverty. This is the chief reason for the low key scholastic performance of scheduled caste women. Singh further justifies,

"Academic achievement is positively correlated with intelligence, and intelligence is adversely influenced by social disadvantages." (Amar Kumar Singh 1980). Usha Sree also confirms these findings from her comparison of 300 socially advantage and 300 socially disadvantaged school students. She says that the socially disadvantaged group was inferior in scholastic achievement and academic adjustment. Academic adjustment significantly influenced scholastic achievement.

Table 12.6 and 12.7 establishes the fact that even though a very large number of respondents were aware of the reservation of seats for scheduled caste quite a sizable number of them concede that they were unaware of the facilities offered to them. The accuracy of knowledge about this fact was mainly regarding (1) educational facilities (2) fee concessions and (3) reservation in government offices.

There were 17 per cent to 28 per cent of respondents from the four centres who had not taken any cognisance of this policy. Similarly from three centres—Bombay (17.33%), Pune (35%) and

Table 12.6

Respondents' Knowledge about Reservation of Seats for Scheduled Castes

Did you know about reservation of seats When you were taking education	*Bombay*	*Pune*	*Nagpur*	*Aurangabad*
Yes	196 (65.33)	156 (52.00)	196 (65.33)	218 (72.66)
No	92 (30.66)	141 (47.00)	102 (34.00)	79 (26.33)
Do not Remember	—	—	—	1 (0.33)
No Reply	11 (3.98)	3 (1.00)	2 (0.66)	2 (0.66)
Total	300 (99.97)	300 (99.99)	300 (99.99)	300 (99.98)

Table 12.7

Knowledge Regarding Reservation of Seats for Scheduled Castes

In what way were you aware of reservations	*Bombay*	*Pune*	*Nagpur*	*Aurangabad*
Fee Concession	28 (9.33)	28 (9.33)	37 (12.33)	55 (18.33)
Free Uniform	2 (0.66)	1 (0.33)	1 (0.33)	4 (1.33)
Free Books	—	1 (0.33)	—	2 (0.66)
Government of India Scholarship	—	3 (1.00)	12 (4.00)	47 (15.66)
Educational facilities	149 (49.66)	93 (31.00)	115 (38.33)	120 (40.00)
Fee concession + Educational facilities	1 (0.33)	13 (4.33)	6 (2.00)	—
Reservation in Government offices	18 (6.00)	5 (1.66)	5 (1.66)	—
Not taken	50 (16.66)	51 (17.00)	84 (28.00)	72 (24.00)
No Reply	52 (17.33)	105 (35.00)	40 (13.33)	—
Total	300 (99.97)	300 (99.98)	300 (99.98)	300 (99.98)

Nagpur (13.33%) there was no reply to this query from the respondents. This shows the failure on the part of the authorities regarding the percolation of information to the Scheduled Castes who can benefit from the schemes.

From Table 12.8, we find that a major group receives educational facilities, another large group gets a full freeship, while a few get combination of benefits such as full freeship and educational facilities. This should have encouraged them to do better. Unfortunately it has not been so. Giving of additional incentives for better performance, such as cash prizes for the good students, assurance of free hostel accommodation in good universities would be a challenge for better work performance. These students if they are encouraged to intermix with other caste students, it may fire their imagination for scholastic achievement. This will open the scheduled caste students eyes to the fact that other students have to work very hard to get admission to professional institutions, for freeships, and get prizes etc. whereas the scheduled castes normally get these under protective discrimination. This additional incentive would benefit the truly intelligent scheduled caste students to achieve on scholastic ability and develop values of self confidence based on hard work and merit.

Table 12.8

Respondents' Receiving Scheduled Castes Benefits

Did you get concession in fees ?	*Bombay*	*Pune*	*Nagpur*	*Aurangabad*
Yes	248 (82.66)	270 (90.00)	271 (90.33)	234 (78.00)
No	46 (15.33)	29 (9.66)	26 (8.67)	64 (21.33)
Do not Remember	—	—	1 (0.33)	—
Not taken	—	1 (0.33)	—	—
No Reply	6 (2.00)	—	2 (0.66)	2 (0.66)
Total	300 (99.99)	300 (99.99)	300 (99.99)	300 (99.99)

Financial Aids

Besides scholarships and freeships, educating girls requires considerable finances for their maintenance. In India this financial burden has to be borne by the family members as there are no other avenues of earnings. In the case of our respondents the financial burden for higher education is borne by;

(*i*) their parents

(*ii*) a few have been helped by relatives

(*iii*) a few got the scholarship and were aided by

parents when required (Table 12.9). Only a negligible number took a part time job and some helped themselves by doing odd jobs during vacation. This is rather surprising as it indicates a lack of achievement drive among the respondents. This may be due to reasons such as:

(*i*) not having a reference group to emulate and get over behaviour problems,

(*ii*) not wanting to work hard for achievement but complacency with their position,

(*iii*) they are assured of some job by virtue of being scheduled caste.

Table 12.9

Financial Aid for Education

Who financed your education?	*Bombay*	*Pune*	*Nagpur*	*Aurangabad*
Parents	181 (60.33)	250 (83.33)	206 (68.67)	106 (33.33)
Help from relatives	30 (10.00)	12 (4.00)	13 (4.34)	63 (21.00)
Part time job	4 (1.33)	1 (0.33)	3 (1.00)	12 (4.00)
Scholarship and parents	81 (27.00)	37 (12.33)	74 (24.66)	114 (38.00)
Other means	—	—	—	—
Parents and Husband	—	—	3 (1.00)	—
Self	1 (0.33)	—	—	1 (0.33)
Parents and relatives	3 (1.00)	—	—	4 (1.33)
No Reply	—	—	1 (0.33)	—
Total	300 (99.99)	300 (99.99)	300 (99.99)	300 (99.99)

Our analysis is applicable only to respondents who pursued higher education—beyond SSC. What we have so far observed is regarding college and university education. Higher education requires deferred gratification and motivation as scheduled caste women can easily get a job after SSC. There are 'earn and learn' schemes in plentiful for these women, which could be taken advantage of, yet very few seemed to pay attention to these facilities.

These attitudes must be discouraged for regularization of people and methods of getting over caste barriers are very important. One must realize that in the attempt to equalize the status and opportunities of people in India and by creating protective discrimination another type of inequality has been created. The scheduled caste must be propelled towards, (1) self respect, (2) self-sufficiency, (3) spirit of competitive effort, (4) achievement drive. Protective discrimination does not initiate these values for scheduled caste become more dependent on aid than over. This may be because of the dire poverty and other socio-economic handicaps. We saw the affect of aid on the respondents. Though a sizable number had no difficulty in getting aid from government 26 per cent from Bombay, 13 per cent from Pune 19 per cent, from Nagpur and 36 per cent from Aurangabad did face difficulties in receiving financial aid given by government. This must have been truly a harassing experience as well as harrowing one as their very existence depended on the aid given by government.

Though the respondents had to face some difficulty in receiving aid from the government their feeling about accepting this aid was mixed. A overwhelming majority of respondents—90 per cent from Bombay, 94 per cent from Pune, 96 per cent from Nagpur and 99 per cent from Aurangabad did not feel ashamed or degrading to accept the freeship. In fact from the responses we find that a large group from among these respondents felt it was their birth right to get such aid from the government.

Other difficulties for pursuing education as ranked by the respondent have been tabulated in Table 12.10. The respondents believed that because of their socio-economic position and inadequate help from government, they could not afford to buy all the books hence their performance suffered. They also believed that instructions of English as a subject was difficult to follow. A few have also said that they were under great stress as they did not receive the scholarship in time. Financial constraints and the uncertainty of receiving them resulted in lack of

Table 12.10

Respondent's Difficulties

Type of difficulties faced by the respondents	*Bombay*	*Pune*	*Nagpur*	*Aurangabad*
Could not afford to buy all the book	117 (39.00)	76 (25.33)	119 (39.66)	114 (38.00)
Instructions through English were difficult to follow	51 (17.00)	27 (9.00)	34 (11.33)	23 (7.66)
Non-receipt of scholarship in time	27 (9.00)	9 (3.00)	22 (7.33)	9 (3.00)
Not getting proper food	8 (2.66)	6 (2.00)	10 (3.33)	7 (2.33)
Economizing on other needs because of inadequate scholarship	10 (3.33)	8 (2.66)	23 (7.66)	39 (13.00)
Negligence towards studies due to worries and mental disturbance due to lack of finances	25 (8.34)	12 (4.00)	27 (9.00)	96 (32.00)
No difficulties	40 (13.33)	153 (51.00)	42 (14.00)	5 (1.66)
None of these	10 (3.33)	5 (1.66)	21 (7.00)	6 (2.00)
No Reply	12 (4.00)	4 (1.33)	2 (0.66)	1 (0.33)
Total	300 (99.99)	300 (99.98)	300 (99.97)	300 (99.98)

concentration and average marks. A few have also felt that they had to economise on other needs because of inadequate scholarship. There has been a large enough group for us to take notice of—who have said that their performance suffered due to negligence towards studies due to worries and mental disturbance due to lack of finances.

The scheduled caste women's merit position inspite of 37 years of reservation remained rather dissatisfactory. What then was the reason for it? Was it due to inability to study properly or due to financial constraints?

Table 12.11

Reasons for Finding Studies Difficult

Reasons	*Bombay*	*Pune*	*Nagpur*	*Aurangabad*
Because of English Medium	70 (23.33)	37 (12.33)	62 (20.66)	79 (26.33)
No guidance	163 (54.33)	103 (34.33)	164 (54.66)	167 (55.67)
Due to heavy syllabus could not pay enough attention	38 (12.66)	25 (8.34)	34 (11.33)	25 (8.34)
No difficulties	14 (4.66)	130 (43.44)	33 (11.0)	23 (7.66)
No Interest	1 (0.33)	1 (0.33)	—	—
2 and 3 above	1 (0.33)	1 (0.33)	1 (0.33)	—
All 1 + 2 + 3	12 (4.00)	3 (1.00)	4 (1.33)	—
No Reply	1 (0.33)	—	2 (0.66)	—
Total	300 (99.97)	300 (99.99)	300 (99.97)	300 (99.99)

Table 12.11 gives us the reasons for finding studies difficult. The chief reason seems to be lack of guidance. A few thought that because of English medium instructions at college level they were not able to perform well. A few could not cope with the syllabus as it was too heavy and they could not give it enough attention. None of the other caste students ever vocalized that the syllabus was heavy.

One of the major reasons is that these respondents lacked a climate of education in their families. As the mother who is a major socializer in the family, was illiterate or barely literate the importance and prestige of education was lost on them. Here the policy of reservation has failed completely. The incentive to select more women from reserved categories for higher education would have given us a better educated number of Scheduled Class people by now. Gandhiji's observation that when a man is educated it is for his own betterment, but when a women is educated, the benefits acrue to the entire family.

Conclusion

Even after 49 years of independence school drop-outs continue to persist amongst scheduled castes, because of non-perception of functional utility of education. To sum up we can say that school drop outs are due to:

(i) a widening gap of knowledge,

(ii) external constraints in the form of incapacity for differed gratification,

(iii) socio-economic factor that turn even a child an economic asset, and a bread winner. (This is in many cases due to extreme poverty),

(iv) cultural factor which contributes to the belief,

- *(a)* that the child is entering school at an age when he should play,
- *(b)* the present system do not allow a child to train himself for a suitable vocation.

(v) *(a)* defective educational system, that is believed to be delinked from the pattern of life.

(*b*) lack of attention paid to individual students in single teacher and over-crowded schools.

(*c*) lack of incentive on the part of the students and motivation on the part of the parents.

Can this School Drop-out Syndrome be Checked?

There definitely can be remedies for this malady. We shall try to enlist a few corrective measures.

(1) Although all the groups of children are exposed to the same teaching learning situations—it is in-advisable to have the same patented text book. The existing text books first of all must be replaced. For example, the standardized text books begins with 'A' for Apple ... 'R'—Railway or 'T'—Television or Telephone. This rigid pattern is the first stumbling block. For these examples of introducing alphabets is not conceivable to a scheduled caste or a rural child due to the lack of cultural context of the book. Thus these books lack the associative links. Though they are excellent for urbanites—may be even to the slum dwellers, but not for the scheduled caste children living in rural areas. Our sample shows 50 per cent of the respondents had migrated to urban centres from rural areas after their education. The books are generally written by urbanites and they are not aware of the difficulties of the scheduled caste. More interesting fare could entice even the most reluctant student to the class room.

(2) An incentive in the form of free books, food and clothing to the scheduled caste child would be useful, but should not be freely available. Some work in turn should be extracted from them in the nature of vocational training with in the available natural resources. Even if the children do not complete entire formal schooling, this vocational training would be an additional means of supplementing income in later life. Thus another important value is inculcated into them that of the dignity of labour. Children who cannot comprehend gains of formal education, would feel pleasure, according to their value system, for having created something worthwhile in economic terms. Absenteeism will also be reduced if the regular students carry home some monetary gain whereas the absentees will not get any remuneration.

(3) The scheduled caste children from rural areas monetary consideration would keep the children in the class room by giving them work oriented courses and a paid compensation for it. This will serve as an incentive to the parents to send their children to schools.

(4) Greater advantage could be taken to the ability to understand scientific concepts amongst the scheduled caste by planning massive community programmes with a view to change the aspirational levels of the disadvantaged children.

(5) The school could go to the children in rural areas or slums. A mobile school room would be ideal. The teachers will have to be especially attentive to socially disadvantaged children.

(6) A creche attached to the school may lighten the domestic burden of the school girls. Special educational projects based on audio-visual programmes could be designed to bridge the widening gap in knowledge of the scheduled caste and rural children.

The drop out in the primary stage no doubt, increase illiterate children. These children in time become illiterate adults. As a result the social perception level of these adults is much lower than those who are educated. The collective representation of ideas, beliefs and values held in common by this group of society contribute very little to social change. We naturally expect that ideas beliefs and values would regulate life in an industrial or even in an agrarian civilization due to the influence of modern ideological changes. But these changes seem to take a very very long time to affect the life of the illiterates. This we feel is because majority miss the education and have a static attitude towards social change. Thus we find that social change takes a considerable time to percolate into Indian society. We therefore, believe that the key to change and improvement in status of girls is dependent on education. So the responsibility rests on Government to reduce drop-outs from schools effectively This would contribute to the economic development and social change in the society.

The conclusions from the data of the educated employed scheduled caste women would give us grounds to suggest remedial measures.

(I) The reasons for educating the respondents by parents was chiefly:

(a) to raise income earning capacity,

(b) to get knowledge,

(c) for personal development, and

(d) to get a white collar job.

(II) The respondents reasons for taking higher education was:

(a) for employment,

(b) education a goal of life,

(c) for getting higher status in society,

(d) for economic security,

(e) for improving the standard of the family.

(III) Most of the respondents had a second class at the SSC level, a second class at undergraduate level, those who went to college also got a second class at the graduate level. Respondents have also got a second class in the diploma exam and also at the post graduate level. Very few got a merit scholarship distinction or a first class in their scholastic career.

(IV) Most of the respondents were aware about reservation of seats for the scheduled caste. The greatest number were aware about:

(a) Educational facilities,

(b) fee concessions,

(c) reservations in government office for scheduled caste people.

(V) A large number did not have any problems in receiving financial aid from government sources. However, 36 per cent of the respondents from Aurangabad and 26 per cent of Bombay respondents said that they had trouble receiving the government aid.

(VI) The respondents were equivocal in confessing that they had no qualms in accepting financial aid from the government. In fact they opine that it is their right to get such aid.

(VII) The difficulties faced by respondents due to poverty were inability to buy all the books, non-receipt of scholarship in time, not able to get proper food.

(VIII) The reasons for finding studies difficult in the majority of cases was lack of guidance followed by difficulty of English and heavy course content.

(IX) A majority found it essential to take help in their studies. Nearly 1/3rd of the respondents took help from their teachers and higher caste friends while others took help from elder brother, sister, mother and father who ever was educated and willing to help.

(X) The reasons for not seeking help was because of:

(a) feeling of inferiority,

(b) could not take tuitions because of economic reasons,

(c) non-co-operation of teachers, inferiority about their language, and

(d) fear of being insulted.

(XI) Majority of the respondents felt that there was no discrimination from teachers in their attitude to them. But a few (20%) felt that teachers were harsh towards scheduled caste women. Equal number opined that they were very considerate. This shows that the teachers harshness or consideration may be based mainly on the student's performance.

(XII) Most of the students said that there were less than ten scheduled caste students in their class.

In this paper we have thoroughly examined the pattern of school drop out amongst scheduled caste women in Maharashtra and also at those employed women who have the minimum qualifications for a white collared job.

The Government's measures of protective discrimination have not benefited the scheduled caste women as much as was expected. The reservations were not implemented on the basis of sex. Scheduled caste women have been the relatively late comers in the field of education because of the 'double-bind' of being women and scheduled caste at that.

Even though compensatory discrimination provides for higher education, it has not been taken by women as they could get jobs, immediately after the completion of the school leaving certificate. So we find majority of our respondents were only SSC passed. We can then infer to an extent the compelling equalities have indirectly reduced the incentive for higher education. Women from the scheduled castes could not wait for deferred gratification and spend some time in college to attain greater scholastic abilities.

Since scheduled caste women respondents belong to low profile families, we find no motivation for achievement in education. Only because of protective discrimination, they could get the jobs, which in a way reduce competition and spirit of achievement.

We have noticed scheduled caste women infinitesimally small in number in Government/Public Sector undertakings in comparison to scheduled caste men. They did not get entry into private sector white collar employment, which is based on rational criteria of attainment.

The scheduled caste women who are in fact the second earning member in the family, still feel that their children should get reservations in education and job even though they now belong to middle class families, who can afford to educate their children. This compensatory discrimination idea has taken deep roots into their psyche and they want it to be extended without any time limit.

The aim of education according to these women is like any other middle class women wherein they perceive education as a means for white collared employment. This functional interpretation of education is a trend towards modernization. We must point out certain loop holes in the implementation of the policies of reservations and free education, to prevent wastage of resources. Unless the government tries to reduce the school drop-outs to a minimum level, they cannot hope to bring the scheduled caste into the mainstream of Indian society.

Women have realized the importance of functional education while the government planners have not given adequate consideration to this aspect. Unless all scheduled caste women who complete education get a job, there would be no motivation for future generations to strive for higher education.

Suggestions

We would like to advocate a policy of 'reservation within a reservation'. As scheduled caste women are 50 per cent of the scheduled caste population, they should get 50 per cent of the seats in higher education and 50 per cent of seats in jobs.

As education of a woman brings out change of the entire family, scheduled caste girls education should be taken up on a war footing if the unnatural protective discrimination has to come to an end within twenty-five years.

Some prizes or cash incentives should be given to girls who complete their ten years of education and a punitive measure of collecting a fine from the parents who stop the education of their wards before they completed SSC.

BIBLIOGRAPHY

1. Abbasayulu, Y.B., 1978, Scheduled Caste Elite, Department of Sociology, Osmania University, Hyderabad.
2. Atal Yogesh, 1968, The Changing Frontiers of Caste National, Delhi.
3. Brembeck, Cole, S., 1966, Social Foundations of Education Across Cultural Approach John Wiley and Sons, New York.
4. Buchman, I.A. 1972, Youngmen in High School and Beyond: A Summary of Finding from the Youth in transition Project. Memographed Report, Survey Research Centre, Institutre of Social Reseach, University of Michigan, USA.
5. Chauhan, Brij Raj and Narayan G., 1976, Problems of Education Among Scheduled Castes students in Utter Pradesh, New Delhi, Social Change.
6. Chitnis, Suma, 1981, A Long Way to Go, New Delhi, ICSSR, Allied Publishers Private Ltd.
7. Dratt Sixth Five Year Plan, 1978-83; 1977, Revised, New Delhi, Government of India, Planning Commission.

8. Education at a Glance, 1983, Poona, Directorate of Education, Maharashtra State.

9. Sixth Five Year Plan of India, Government of India, 1981.

10. Mankidy Aruna; 1979, Social Change, New Delhi, Inter Generational Occupational Mobility Among the Scheduled Castes.

11. Manning, Nash; 1971, 'The Role of Village School in the Process of Cultural and Economic Modernization' in Gezi, Kalil (Ed.) Education in Comparative and International Perspective, New York, Holt, Kineharet and Winston.

12. Naidu, U.S., 1979, Social Change, New Delhi, Socialization of Scheduled Caste Children at School.

13. Naik, J.P., 1978, Equality, Quality and Quantity, Delhi, Allied Publishers.

14. Pande, Namita; 1980, Irregular Attendance at School: Elimate Support to Scheduled Caste Students, Social Change, New Delhi, Vol. 10, No. 1 & 2.

15. Rao, Usha, 1981, Deprived Castes in India, Chugh Publications, Allahabad.

16. Rathnaiah E.V. 1977, Social Constraints in Tribal Education, A Regional Study; Sterling Publishers Private Ltd., Delhi.

17. Rath, R. 1974, Teaching and Learning Problems of the Disadvantaged Children.

18. Report of the Commissioner for Scheduled Castes, and Scheduled Tribes, Part I, 1975-77, New Delhi.

19. Report of the Commissioner for Scheduled Castes and Scheduled Tribes, Part II, 1978-79.

20. Sachiachet, P.J., 1975, Identity Conflicts in Minority College Youth, Journal of Contemporary Psychology, Vol. 17, pp. 134-38.

21. Sapra, C.L., Educational Wastage and Stagnation, India, New Delhi, NCERT, 1967.

22. Singh Amar Kumar, 1980, Social Disadvantage and Academic Achievement, Social Change, Vol. 10, No. 1 & 2.

23. Singh, T.P., Pandey, B.P., Dubey, G.S. and Yadava, D.R., 1976, Social Change, New Delhi, Educational Aspirations of Scheduled Castes Students in Uttar Pradesh.

24. Trivedi Harshad, 1977, Scheduled Caste Women, Concept, New Delhi.

25. Ushasree, S. 1980, Social Disadvantage, Academic Adjustment and Socialistic Achievement, Social Change, Vol. 10, No. 1 & 2.

13

Women in Men's World: The Anatomy of Leadership

Women may be more publicly visible now than in the past, but it is misleading to assume that there is a specific form of leadership practised by "women as leaders" or "women in management." To label managers or leaders as special because they are women is itself part of the problem of the unequal social conditions of the sexes.

The Social and Economic Context

The distribution of women and men in organizations takes a wide range of historical and cultural forms [1]. In many societies women have been, and are, the predominant producers of food, although their proportion of the community's wealth is small and they have less access to literacy and other sources and signs of public power. Historically, women have frequently had multiple responsibilities and therefore leadership roles, including home production of goods, teaching, healing, and agriculture. Novarra [2] identifies the following major tasks that have traditionally constituted "women's work" in Western society: bearing children, providing and preparing food, providing clothing, tending the sick and frail, early education, organizing the house, and emotional support work. In recent centuries such activities have become incorporated into public organizations, factories, schools, hospitals, and other male-dominated bureaucracies [3]. Women still continue in their traditional family and caring roles, but no longer have control over them.

Abundant evidence is now available to confirm that women tend to occupy less-powerful, lower-paid, and lower-status organizational positions than men. This not only can be seen in a mass of census and other official sources, including the various state "equal opportunity" agencies, but is analyzed in great detail in a large number of texts focusing on such topics as "the sexual division of labour," women and work," and "the sexual structuring of organization."[1]

The broad and pronounced tendency for men to occupy official leadership positions—in terms of *organizational role* at least—results from many factors and forces both outside and inside organizations. These include the domination of the public over the private domain, production over reproduction, and paid work over domestic and unpaid work. In addition, some commentators consider that women and men are a part of a dual labour market [4], women being part of a "reserve army of labour" [5, 6], performing "dual roles" as paid workers and domestic child-carers, and even "triple roles" as carers also of the elderly and infirm. Within organizations, relevant factors and forces include the valuation of men as intellectual workers over women as manual workers [7], of men as professionals over women as semi-or paraprofessionals [8], of men as manual workers in "nondomestic" trades—for example, engineering—over women as manual workers in "domestic" trades—for example, in clothing industries [9, 10]—of men as full-time workers over women as part-time workers [11], and even of men as registered unemployed workers over women who are not registered as unemployed. Such divisions between women and men in the official organizational designation of leaders and leadership are frequently reflected in informal relations between women and men [12]. Leadership as a process between women and men has both formal and informal elements.

Divisions between women and men within organizations apply not only vertically, in terms of authority and types of labour, but also laterally, horizontally or spatially. Leadership roles can be conceptualized as part of the centre or core of organizational activity, while other roles can be seen as part of the periphery, as boundary roles. Frequently this "spatial" distance between centre and periphery in organizational structuring and in leadership involves clear divisions between men and women. In some organizations part of the leadership role of men comprises the direction of women into boundary roles that the men do not consider leadership roles. Ironically, such boundary roles may demand considerable initiative from workers and even involve high degrees of autonomy [13], qualities that might elsewhere be labelled those of leadership.

Furthermore, just as there may often be divisions between men at the centre of organizations and women at the boundary, there may be similar divisions between those within and those outside organizations, as customers, clients, or other members of the public. Although it is, of course, difficult to generalize about the various clienteles of organizations, many organizations are characterized by clear differences between the distribution of women and men on and around the "front line." This can occur between male professionals and female clients, for example, in gynecological settings, or between female receptionists and male customers. When jobs as secretaries, receptionists, or salespersons in boutiques are allocated to women as a matter of course, they may involve women's being employed to sell their sexuality as part of their labour power [14].

The essential point is that the conceptualization and evaluation of leadership *within* organizations and management often parallel or accompany *inverse* conceptualizations and evaluations of what is seen as nonleadership at or around the organizational boundary. In this way divisions between women and men—as, say, receptionists and clients—may reinforce leadership patterns, especially when the selling of sexuality is viewed as indicating the opposite of leadership. In contrast, leadership is usually understood as "a sexual," "neutral," or, above all, male.

Traditional Leadership

It is within the above-described general social and economic context that dominant traditional forms and notions of leadership have developed, both theoretically and practically. Characteristically, leadership has been performed by men; and characteristically, notions of leadership have implicitly assumed that leaders are to be men. Hence, leadership may be assumed to imply maleness, and maleness may be assumed to carry with it inherent qualities of leadership that women lack. These particular shortcomings of prevailing notions are obscured by a general lack of attention to the study of women and men within organizations [15].

A major example of these assumptions is Weber's three ideal-typical forms of authority [16]. First, leadership may be seen as arising from the traditional authority that comes from a socially accepted status, as, for example, that of fathers. Second, leadership may be understood as the product of the qualities and charisma of "great men." Third, leadership may be taken for granted as the usual complement of rational-legal authority within bureaucracies.

Although these interpretations are distinct within Weber's theorizing, elements of all three can be discerned in many mainstream studies of, and prescriptions for, leadership—for example, Taylor's "management of men" [17]. Subsequent work within organizational psychology attempted to identify the most significant traits in the selection and performance of leaders [18]. The major synthesis of these approaches is to be found in the social systems theories of Parsons, Bales, and colleagues [19,20] in terms of types of behaviour. Such studies not only presumed the importance of role differentiation between women and men but frequently noted the pro-active competence of men over and against women [21]. Although much of this research was conducted in small-group contexts [22], the impact of its assumptions on organization theory and management theory has been lasting.

Even studies that are critical of the traits approach (*e.g.*, Bavelas [23]) or are at pains to point out the dysfunction and incompetence of rigid leadership (*e.g.*, Dixon [24], on the British army) often convey the assumption that leaders are to be men. The accompanying observations concerning women at the bottom of, at the boundaries of, or beyond organizations often bear the implicit assumption that women have inherent qualities of submissiveness that necessitate their being led by men. Classic studies in which such divisions of men as leaders and women as subordinates are not seen as problematic include Mayo's investigation of the Western Electric Company [25] and Crozier's analysis of French bureaucracy [26].

Variations in leadership style, from authoritarian to more participatory stances [27], are subtle variations on a masculine theme. Within many models of leadership, the necessary and desirable qualities are assumed to be masculine. This assumption is deeply entrenched in thinking and language, so that the language of leadership often equates with the language of masculinity to include qualities such as aggression, assertiveness, abrasiveness, and competitiveness. When women demonstrate such qualities and become leaders, a distortion of the language often occurs: aggressive becomes "overdomineering," and assertive is viewed as bossy and strident. Even more pejorative terms are used to describe men who demonstrate a different style of leadership, one that may be seen as more flexible and co-operative: they may be subject to derogatory comments ascribing supposedly feminine attributes to their leadership. In such an ideological perspective, leadership is not considered a female occupation, a female leader is regarded as an aberration, and women who become leaders are often offered the presumed accolade of being described as being like men.

The Entry of Women into Management

The growth of hierarchical bureaucracies has produced a situation in which, it can be argued, there is little distinction between formal leadership and management. Males continue to dominate in such organizations, women seldom gaining top management posts and being grossly underrepresented even in lower management positions. This applies not only to technological and engineering organizations but also to educational and welfare organizations, in which women often predominate in numerical terms.

The slow increase in the number of women in management, or attempting to become part of management, has produced a considerable literature, particularly in the United States, offering both theoretical interpretations and practical advice (*e.g.*, Gordon and Strober [28], Fenn [29], Stead [30]). Excellent bibliographies on "women in management" are contained in Stead and in Leavitt [31].

In much of this literature there is a concern with the entry of women into management. For example, Hennig and Jardim's [32] advice for the aspiring careerist women in management is to bear in mind that she is "... going to a foreign country for an extended stay." In a foreign country one has to learn, or at least try to use, a foreign language and understand different norms and standards. In the case of management, women are entering a well-established male preserve with well-established rules and language. These circumstances can be important determinants of female behaviour. An interesting variant on these *corporate* dynamics is provided by the managerial experiences of women as *entrepreneurs.* Goffee and Scase [33] have recently surveyed British women proprietors and concluded, from the variety of their experiences, that they can be "innovative entrepreneurs," "conventional businesswomen," "radical co-owners," or "domestic traders."

In contrast, the entry of men into management is taken for granted: they are already there; some may even assume that it is an inherent attribute of men that they should be there. Thus, in subtle ways the conceptualization of the entry of women into management can reinforce the equation of leadership with masculinity.

The phenomenon of women in management raises the further question of whether those women, once they have "entered" management, have a different style of leadership, stemming from the supposedly inherent qualities of women. The "sex differences" approach to women in management assumes that women possess characteristic qualities which result in a form of leadership different from that of men. Women's qualities in leadership can then be used or exploited in an organization, perhaps in an attempt to "soften" its image [34]. Another "sex differences" approach argues that women who achieve leadership have denied or repressed the attributes of their sex and have become like men.

Jacklin and Maccoby [35] have looked critically at sex differences and their implications for management. Their research provides little evidence for substantiating a "sex differences" approach, pointing out, for example, that "The male potential for empathic and sympathetic emotional reactions and male potential for kindly helpful behaviour towards others (including children) is seriously underrated". They also put the issue in a broader context, nothing: "... dominance or leadership appears to be achieved primarily by aggressive means among apes and little boys. Among human beings, the linkage weakens with increasing maturity and there appears to be no intrinsic reason why the more aggressive sex should be the dominant one in adult relations". No evidence of sex differences was found in achievement motivation, risk-taking, task persistence, or other, related skills. Jacklin and Maccoby conclude that women are not psychologically handicapped for management, but are blocked by recruitment, hiring, and promotion policies.

Meeker and Weitzel-O' Neill [36] have also comprehensively argued against the sex differences approach and instead propose an analysis of sex roles that is more specifically context based. This may help to describe (though not explain) how status and power are still bestowed on male professionals and managers, whereas status and negative connotations are given to the leadership role of women in the family. Yet, when management courses were set up for women within the University of Aston's Women and Work Programme in England, women came with trepidation, but were amazed to discover that many of the tasks they had been performing might be defined as management functions, though they lacked the social and economic status [37].

Women who seek to enter management clearly face a number of problems. These include coping with additional family and domestic roles [38, 39], managing conflicts between paid work and unpaid work, and fighting against a variety of myths that persist about women's "management potential." The tensions and conflicts women managers face have been a major focus of recent British research on women in management. This work represents an important contribution to the literature and a rather different emphasis from the often more organization-focused American research.

In what is the most sophisticated analysis yet of women in management, Marshall [40] effectively demystifies and counters the following six such misapprehensions, drawing on published research evidence:

(1) Women are different from men, so they do not make good managers.
(2) Women do not have the same motivations towards work as men.
(3) Stereotypes of women mean companies are reluctant to employ them as managers.
(4) Women believe the stereotypes too, and behave accordingly.
(5) Other people will not work for or with women, or make life difficult for them if they do.
(6) When women go out to work their children and husbands and homes suffer, and society suffers as a result.

It is not surprising that therefore in such a social context, women managers experience considerable pressures and stress [41, 42]. More positively, it can be argued that the dual roles and multiple responsibilities of women mean that they are *more* eminently suited for the multiple responsibilities of management, as they have wider experience of complexity and decision making in different settings. Furthermore, these complications and potentialities have important consequences for the training of women—and, indeed, men—managers. Recent discussions of such issues are to be found in an Irish study of the problems of women and men working together [43] and Dutch experience of women—only training in the face of some women's isolation and difficulty in entering into open conflict in a constructive manner [44].

Although most of the literature dealing with the entry of women into management stands in clear opposition to traditional assumptions about leadership and its domination by males, it can itself be criticized as limited in certain respects. The literature on women in management is predominantly business oriented, American in origin and in cultural assumptions, often unduly optimistic about the immediate possibilities for change, and devoted to what remains an issue for a relative minority of women. It seems to obscure various issues that affect most women, such as whether the presence of more women managers would improve the lot of women workers. The literature is often psychological in orientation, stressing the "managerial qualities" of particular women and rarely considering the larger questions of social structure and power. It does not necessarily provide a general, critical reformulation of the relationship of gender and leadership, as management is usually assumed to involve a relatively fixed set of powers and practices that women may assume and apply.

Leadership as Processes Between Women and Men

In contrast to viewing management and leadership as something performed by managers or leaders *upon* others who are managed or led, one may conceptualize them as processes *between* people, in this context, women and men. If management and leadership are processes as well as practices, this means that it is equally important to consider the effects of leaders upon the led and the led upon leaders—and indeed, the relations between the two groups. It may even be necessary to question the usefulness of the terms *leaders* and *led*. For example, Whyte's [45] classic study of the social structure of the restaurant suggests that leadership roles of male kitchen staff are based on taking responsibility for originating initiatives *for* women. The male kitchen staff has much to gain by containing orders (both for food and in general) from female waitresses by physical barriers, use of written slips, and generally setting their own pace of work.

The interesting point is that leadership is no longer the province of one set of (male) leaders, but involves all organizational members, with reciprocal yet partial attempts to influence and control overtures made by others, both women and men, in the organization. This occurs within a more general process that cannot be determined by any one group or set of leaders.

Subsequent American studies of women's and men's leadership in a variety of group situations also emphasize the importance of looking at the reciprocal behaviour of "leaders" and "nonleaders," superordinates and subordinates, women and men, at the same time [46]. The research in this area is complex, but a number of examples will give some idea of the type of questions that have been addressed.

Bartol [47] has noted the adverse effects of male leaders on female group members' satisfaction with task structure, compared with the mildly positive effect on task situations of female leaders for female followers in mixed groups. It is no longer possible to consider the evaluation of female or male leaders in isolation. Another study, by Bartol and Wortman [48], takes the analysis of these processes further in concluding that although leaders' sex may be a significant factor in determining, *inter alia,* perceived leader behaviour or job satisfaction, the nonleader's sex may be significant in determining how the leader is perceived and the nonleader's own job satisfaction. A more recent, critical study, by Mayes [49], has examined the differences in the reactions of women and men nonleaders within female- and male-led groups. The reactions were found to be to the whole group process, not just to the leader. Men's reactions to female-led groups were particularly interesting: they included feelings of hostility, dependency, confusion, and, above all, uncomfortableness.

Authority and Power Relations

A process approach to leadership may emphasize informal relations, but has clear implications for formal structuring. Simpson and Simpson [8], for example, postulate that the differences in work orientation of women and men may be a major factor in the tendency of numerically female-dominated organizations, such as in the "semiprofessions" of teaching, nursing, social work, and librarianship, to become more bureaucratic and more centralized. Sexual divisions can account for a particular type of formal process of authority and leadership. Although their work has subsequently been criticized, not least on empirical grounds [50, 51], the Simpsons' contribution is a lasting one. They have raised issues and questions on the need to understand patterns and processes of leadership as but one part of a system of authority and power relations between women and men, both inside and outside a given organization.

Thus, as noted above, we may usefully reinterpret aspects of Crozier's [26, 52] classic study of power in the French bureaucracy, and even the Hawthorne Experiments in the Relay Assembly Testing Room [25], as being products of the power relations between men superordinates and women subordinates, as well as of control over uncertainty and informal dynamics.

Kanter [53] has analyzed the distribution of power within organization as a central issue in determining the distribution of work attitudes and behaviour, including leadership, between women and men. She sees the location of a person in the organizational structure as a more significant determinant of leadership behaviour than sex differences per se. Many women and some men are in disadvantaged positions in society and in organizations, but women are the more disadvantaged. The structure of power within organizations rather than gender attributes explains the concentration of women at the bottom of the hierarchy.

Wells [54] argues, similarly, that women have been "late entries" into organizations, whose structure and power relations were already determined by masculine values and male prerogatives. Accordingly, women may often find that the covert power of men, reinforced by the hierarchical power structure of organizations, influences the way in which women experience power. Reducing hierarchical power within hierarchical organizations can thus assist both women and men, but has greater potential for changing the lot of women.

This approach to leadership and its change raises a more subtle issue: that power in organizational settings is itself understood and experienced as essentially male [55]. According to this formulation, not only do men dominate within organizations but they dominate the currency by which domination is maintained. Kanter [56] maintains that subordinates often prefer to work for the "powerful," which in practical evaluations tends to mean men: as she puts it, "preference for men-preference for power." Men's continuing domination of leadership roles, particularly as formal leaders, is only part of the male domination of leadership: in addition, the process of leadership, what counts as leadership, the means of gaining legitimacy in leadership, and so on, are male dominated in most organization.

The Critique of Men

The development of the power perspective on leadership necessarily leads to consideration of the power of men. This perspective from within organization theory links with more broadly based feminist and other critiques. Hence, there is a dual reason for exploring the critique of men.

Feminist and other radical critiques have addressed men's leadership in a number of different ways. First, and most obviously, critiques have been developed in relation to the behaviour of particular men leaders. Pollert [12], for example, in her study of a tobacco factory in Bristol, England, discusses the way in which the authority of male supervisory staff over women workers is maintained and reinforced by sexist language, jokes, and innuendo. Similarly, Kanter [56] and Korda [57] explore the frequent sexism in managers' behaviour. This is particularly crucial for women, such as secretaries, who work closely with managers [58]. More generally still, management, and therefore predominantly male management, can be analyzed as a distinct class-grouping. Management by men can be understood as an important contributory factor to the maintenance of a "capitalist patriarchy" [59].

A second approach to the critique of men is not directed specifically at men who are employed as leaders, but rather at other sources of men's power and leadership at work. Most important of these are the power and leadership that accrue from men's labour power. As Cock burn [60], in her study of the British printing industry, puts it: "The solidarity forget between men as a group of males is part of the organized craft's defence against the employer" This process is important in the development of dominant forms of masculinity among working-class men, which, in turn, has several implications for leadership: perpetuation of the pattern of men as leaders of working-class women, the occasional alliance of male workers with male management, and the general male domination of many organizational cultures.

Third, there are critiques that treat men as a class, and thus represent critiques of men's leadership. The roots of men's being regarded as a class may lie in either biology [61] or the economy, or both. Delphy [62, 63], the French feminist theorist, for example, emphasizes the divisions between women and men in marriage and the family as a mode of production. In such views, ".... every .... relationship [between a women and a man] is a *class* relationship, and the conflicts between individual men and women are political conflicts that can only be resolved collectively" [64]. The relationship between an individual man superordinate and women subordinates, or indeed between a women superordinate and men subordinates, has, from this perspective, to be understood strictly as an instance in a broader class relationship.

Leadership and Sexuality

One specific aspect of leadership that concerns relations between women and men, indeed, between people of the same sex, is sexuality. Men's domination of leadership—in formal, public terms at least—means that many models of masculinity are based on some form of power. Similarly, dominant models of men's sexuality frequently include elements of domination and "mastery." There are numerous detailed ways in which sexuality, power, and leadership can become intertwined [65], in both social and psychological terms [66, 67].

Those in formal positions of leadership may also have either the responsibility for, or an interest in, controlling the sexual behaviour and attitudes of subordinates [68]. This may include taking punitive action against those, particularly women, who engage in sexual liaisons in the organization [69]. Moreover, men managers frequently evaluate women workers not only on the grounds of work done but also of appearance and sexual presentation [70].

Such interest in others' sexual behaviour on the part of leaders may be particularly acute in "total institutions," in which responsibility extends over both staff and inmates. In most organizations, management of sexuality usually involves assumptions of "normality" and, generally, heterosexuality [71]. This can have a wide range of subtle effects on the selection and promotion of leaders and managers—for example, in the evaluation of male executives' wives, and in discrimination against and thus maintenances of, secrecy concerning homosexuality. According to reports from both Britain [72] and Germany [73], the persecution of homosexuality is particularly severe in the armed forces. The implications for leadership styles and the leadership prospects of homosexuals are clear.

These general tendencies within management and leadership sometimes have a greater and more directly oppressive impact on women in the form of sexual harassment. There are now numerous reports of the occurrence of harassment, including that by men managers of subordinate women, and even of women managers and professionals [39, 74]. Surveys in both Britain and the United States have recorded very high rates of sexual harassment of women entering work in jobs not traditionally defined as "women's work" and therefore in relative isolation from other women [75,76]. Such conditions apply to many women in management and other leadership roles, and this raises the question of how men in positions of power may collude with other, less-powerful men in the process of harassment of women.

The significance of sexuality, and indeed of sexual harassment, in leadership is that it represents an incursion of the private into the public domain. It is to this general theme of the public and the private that we now turn

The Public and the Private

Organizations, and therefore leadership in organizational settings, are distributed in a very distinctive way throughout society. Although organizations exist for and across all economic classes and within all spheres of human activity, they are especially prominent in the public domain, which includes most workplaces where people work for payment, political organizations, and public places. Inasmuch as private life does sometimes take place in organizations, *e.g.*, in kibbutzim, and public life does sometimes take place outside organizations, *e.g.*, in crowds and street groups, there is a considerable overlap between the "public" and the "organizational" in most, and particularly Western, societies.

The theme of the public-private divide has been dealt with in recent years by a number of feminist writers, among them O'Brien [77], Elshtain [78], and Stacey and Price [80] at a somewhat theoretical level, and Nowotny [80] and Skard [81] in empirical studies of Austrian and Norwegian women, respectively, O'Brien [82], in particular, has explored the theoretical significance of this divide, arguing that "The opposition of public and private is to the social relations of reproduction what the opposition of economic classes is to the social relations of production."

This perspective is important in understanding both organizations and organizational leadership. It implies that leadership, in organizations at least, usually involves *two* levels of activity and action: first, in the organization concerned, and second, in the public sphere over the private sphere. Not only do women and men tend to occupy positions of leadership unequally in most organizations but there is a further inequality between women and men in terms of the power of the public over the private. Therefore, men usually lead and dominate women not just in particular organizations but also in the way those organizations from part of public life, which is dominated and led by men. For example, male managers may be directly powerful in public, organization settings and indirectly powerful in the private sphere, both with regard to consumers and clients (frequently women) in general and in their own domestic realm.

Several implications follow from this kind of analysis of organization and leadership. One is that particular organizations, and therefore their leadership, can be understood as part of the process of production and/or reproduction. Production and reproduction have very different significance for women and men. This may be a secondary matter within production, even though production taking place in the public sphere may be part of men's domination of women. . Within reproduction, the division between women and men is clearly a primary matter. Thus, for example, leadership, usually by men, in a maternity hospital involves several interrelated elements: the domination of the public over the private, the domination of men over women's reproductive labour [83], and the more specific intraorganizational domination through hierarchy.

Another area of importance in considering the interrelation of women, men, and leadership is in activity on and across the public-private divide. In particular, there are a number of studies stressing the leadership roles of women in moving private experiences, often of other women, into the public, and therefore explicitly political, sphere [84]. Often such pioneering activity is immensely difficult, subject to rapid change and conflicting pressures, and perceived as a threat within male-dominated organizations in the state and elsewhere. A recent British example is the development of the national and local women's aid organizations providing shelter and support for women who have suffered violence from men [85]. Many such initiatives of leadership by women across the public-private divide subsequently encounter attempts by men, often as professionals, to take over or incorporate them [86].

Considerable analytical care needs to be taken in the interpretation of the location of such "peripheral" organizations that stand on or across the public-private divide. Some may represent attempts to establish an autonomous public sphere for women; others may act as subsidiaries of male-dominated organizations, even though they are led by women and perhaps are limited to women members [87]; still others may represent the development of exchange relationships between women in the performance of domestic tasks. Such as "baby-sitting" [88].

Together, such organizational and leadership initiatives, frequently by women, are means of renegotiating the public-private divide.

Comparative Studies

It has been noted a several points in this paper that the dominant tradition in leadership research has been derived from studies in the United States, particularly from American management theory. Accordingly, much of this work is liable to charges of ethnocentrism, especially in the study of gender and leadership. An important development from purely organizational studies of women in management and leadership, reflecting a broadening of questions such as those discussed above, has been an increasing interest in comparative studies of the economic and social positions of women, and thus of men. For example, recent Norwegian studies have noted both wide variations in the cultural forms of, and relation of gender to, leadership [89] and possible variations in conceptions of sex roles even within a particular culture [90]. Cross-cultural and comparative studies are particularly difficult to perform [46], and may indeed fail to yield very firm conclusions [91].

Although most forms of business and managerial leadership are still patriarchal, the precise mechanism for maintaining patriarchal leadership varies considerably. Not only broadly cultural and narrowly organizational factors but also more structural and societal causes of variation must be recognized. Perhaps most important is the impact of past or present feudal structures on industrial and capitalist organizations, as in the Middle East or Japan. For example, Rohlen's study [92] of a large Japanese bank, performed in 1968-69, pointed out that "women must resign on marriage, and there are no exceptions!" In order to achieve senior positions, the few women concerned therefore had to be the appropriate age and unmarried. Although there have been some changes for women since that time, the Japanese system remains paternalistic and patriarchal [93].[2]

Political Leadership

The major contribution of recent comparative studies, and of non-Anglo-American research, has been in analysis of the state of women's participation and representation, or lack of it, in politics and public life rather than specifically in management or business leadership (*pace* Silver [94] and Whitley [95]). This theme is dominant in the important collections edited by Epstein and Coser [96] on elites, Lovenduski and Hills [97] on political participation, and Siltanen and Stanworth [98] on politics in the public sphere. Perhaps the most important point is that what is regarded as "politics" is concerned primarily with men's activities and is generally considered the domain of men, not women, as has been emphasized by the Norwegian commentators Skard [81] and Albrektsen [99].

The Lovenduski and Hills [97] collection, for example, includes surveys of women's public participation in political life in, *inter alia*, Spain (Matsell), Italy (Weber), Sweden (Eduards), Finland (Haavio-Mannila), Eastern Europe (Wolchik), the USSR (Lovenduski), and Japan (Hargadine). These and similar studies consider the extent of women's participation in voting, political party membership and leadership, candidacy and electoral success, and representation in legislatures, governments, and ministerial offices. Sanzone, for instance, reviews the changing representation of women in power positions of central government, particularly their general absence (*pace* Thatcher) from the more prestigious ministries, in France, West Germany, and the United Kingdom.

Although there are gross imbalances in formal political leadership between women and men, it would be a mistake to overgeneralize about their nature, extent, and even causes among different countries and cultures. For example, in the Soviet Union about three-fourths of the doctors are women, but there is not one women in the Politburo. Even within Scandinavia there is considerable cultural variation between the traditionalism of Norway [81] and the relative political activism of Finnish women. A further complication is the impact of various "equal opportunities" and civil rights legislation upon the legal status of women and how this interrelates with leadership practices. The studies we have cited, however, focus on the political leadership of women within male-dominated definitions of politics and organization.

Further Feminist Approaches

Radical feminists such as Siren/Black Rose, Farrow, Kornegger, and Ehrlich go further than this in urging attention to the ideological underpinnings of modern organizations, which they claim are dominated by men. Women's increasing awareness of male supremacy has evoked a variety of responses. Some women have "entered" management and leadership and have demonstrated in ability to perform equally with men in their organizational roles. Far from bringing a "softer" approach, based on supposedly inherent female characteristics of submissiveness, passivity, and caring, to leadership positions, they have demonstrated that women as well as men can be competitive and assertive. This would seem to confirm Kanter's view that organizational position is a more powerful determinant of behaviour and attitude than supposedly inherent sex differences.

Having said that, we have to argue that society does impose on women and men gender roles that inevitably follow them into organizational roles. Thus, women continue to predominate in lower-paid, lower-status, caring roles, often at the bottom of career structures, despite the apparent success of women whose response to male domination has been to campaign for a change in the law that will assure them equal pay and opportunities. Women continue to experience oppression, discrimination, and harassment, and their "entry" into leadership and management and changes in the law have evoked only token responses.

It is not surprising, in view of this, that Charlton, in England, and Gould, in the United States, draw attention to feminist organizations with "non-patriarchal and non-hierarchical" structures that the considered alternatives to the existing male-dominated hierarchies and are not dependent on them. This can imply a "sex differences" approach in which women intrinsically organize themselves co-operatively and non-hierarchically. We have repeatedly argued, however, that the "sex differences" approach is a misleading oversimplification of a complex situation that has its roots in history, tradition, and religion. It ignores women who have successfully risen in hierarchies and men who seek co-operative alternatives. Yet this anti-organizational stance is frequently taken by feminists, who use it not as a statement about the nature of women, but as an illustration of how the sex role assigned to women in our society can be used in a political challenge. This challenge to male power, domination, and leadership can be seen more clearly as a political statement when it is compared with the unwillingness of some black people to reinforce white supremacy by "entering" white organizations and their preference for establishing their own radical alternatives.

A striking example of this sort of political statement in action is the creation of the women's peace movement and the setting-up of peace camps in Britain, and the way they have attracted considerable male hostility and harassment. This reaction suggests that these radical, anti-organization, feminist movements are presenting a stronger challenge to the present male order than does women's joining male-dominated organizations. The former movements represent a double threat to the *status quo* in that they challenge the whole concept of leadership and hierarchy as a form of power and, with it, the long-held view, bound up in all our languages, that leadership, masculinity, and power are inextricably liked. Power becomes "empowerment," "power to" or "power for," not "*power over,*" energy, not domination and thus goes "beyond leadership".

It is therefore appropriate that we conclude with comments from a feminist peace campaigner:

> The male cosmology based on separation and hierarchy gives rise to strategies for peace based on building barriers and creating fear. The result is a never-ending arms spiral. The alternative, a positive peace built on mutual support and co-operation ... It is our vision and our practice of a new way to peace that makes women such an important force in the peace movement—not any "natural pacifism" attributed to women. The common belief that women are by nature non-aggressive is itself part of the female stereotype of passivity, the complement of the idea that violence and war are "natural" to men ... Men are not inherently violent; they are traditionally and structurally dominant and retain that dominance through the cultivation of toughness and violence.

Leadership, as usually understood, is not a natural phenomenon or process; neither is it a natural attribute or possession of women or men; nor is it salvation for either. Leadership needs deconstruction: it is as gendered as it is problematic.

NOTES

1. British material is surveyed by Davies [4] and Mackie and Pattullo [5]; Australian material, by Game and Pringle [6]. Lewenhak [7] takes an admirably international and historical approach, considering the experience of China, France, the United States, and many other countries. Invaluable bibliographies on this material have been prepared by the International Labour Office [8], Winship [9], and Clarricoates, Cooper, and Allen [10].
2. See also the Steinhoff and Tanaka contribution to this volume.

REFERENCES

1. Sanday, P.R. (1981) *Female Power and Male Dominance.* London: Cambridge University Press.
2. Novarra, V. (1980) *Women's Work, Men's Work.* London: Marion Boyars.
3. Ehrenreich, B., and English. D. (1978) *For Her Own Good. 150 Years of Experts' Advice to Women.* New York: Anchor/Doubleday.
4. Barron. R., and Norris. G. (1976) "Sexual Division and the Dual Labour Market." In D. Barker and S. Allen (Eds.), *Dependence and Exploitation in Work and Marriage.* London: Tavistock. pp. 47-69.
5. Braverman. H. (1974) *Labour and Monopoly Capital.* New York: Monthly Review Press.
6. Bruegal, I. (1974) "Women as a Reserve Army of Labour: A Note on Recent British Experience." *Feminist Review, 3,* 12-23.
7. Willis, P. (1977) *Learning to Labour.* Farnborough: Saxon House.
8. Simpson, R.L., and Simpson, I.H. (1969) "Women and Bureaucracy in the Semi-professions." In A. Etzioni (Ed.), *The Semi professions and Their Organization.* New York: The Free Press. pp. 196-65
9. Cunnison, S. (1966) *Wages and Work Allocation.* London: Tavistock.
10. Lupton, T. (1963) *On the Shopfloor.* Oxford: Pergamon.
11. Beynon, H., and Blackburn, R. (1972) *Perceptions of Work. Perceptions within a Factory.* London: Cambridge University Press.
12. Pollert, A. (1981) *Girls, Wives, Factory Lives.* London: Macmillan.
13. Miles, R. (1980) "Organization Boundary Roles." In C. Cooper (Ed.), *Current Issue in Occupational Stress.* Chichester: Wiley. pp. 61-96.
14. Bland, L., Brunsdon, C., Hobson, D., and Winship, J. (1978) "Women 'Inside

and Outside' the Relations of Production." In Women's Studies Group, Centre for Contemporary Cultural Studies, Univeristy of Birmingham, *Women Take Issue.* London: Hutchinson. pp. 35-78.

15. Hearn, J., and Parkin, P.W. (1983) "Gender and Organizations: A Selective Review and a Critique of a Neglected Area." *Organization Studies,* 4(3), 219-42.
16. Weber, M. (1947) *The Theory of Social and Economic Organization.* Glencoe, IL: The Free Press.
17. Taylor, F. (1947) *Scientific Management.* New York: Harper. Section reprinted from Testimony to the House of Representatives Committee, 1912.
18. Stogdill, R. (1948) "Personal Factors Associated with Leadership." *Journal of Psychology, 25,* 35-71.
19. Parsons, T., Bales, R.L., and Shils, E.A. (1951) *Working Papers in the Theory of Action.* Glencoe, IL: The Free Press.
20. Parsons, T., and Bales, R.F. (Eds.) (1955) *Family, Socialization and Interaction.* New York: The Free Press.
21. Strodtbeck, F.L., and Mann, R.D. (1956) "Sex Role Differentiation in Jury Deliberations." *Sociometry, 19,* 3-11.
22. Hare, A.P. (1962) *Handbook of Small Group Research.* Glencoe, IL: The Free Press.
23. Bavelas, A., (1960) "Leadership: Man and Function." *Administrative Science Quarterly,* 4, 491-98.
24. Dixon, N. (1976) *On the Psychology of Military Incompetence.* London: Cape.
25. Mayo, E. (1933) *The Human Problems of an Industrial Civilization* New York: Viking.
26. Crozier, M. (1963) *Le Phenomene Bureaucratique.* Paris: Education du Seuil.
27. Likert, R. (1961) *New Patterns of Management.* New York: McGraw-Hill.
28. Gordon, F., and Strober, M. (Eds.), (1975) *Bringing Women into Management. New York:* McGraw-Hill.
29. Fenn. M. (1978) *Making It in Maanagement.* Englewood Cliffs, NJ: Prentice-Hall.
30. Stead, B.A. (Ed.) (1978) *Women in Management.* Englewood Cliffs, NJ: Prentice-Hall. (2nd ed., 1985).
31. Leavitt, J.A. (1982) *Women in Management: An Annotated Bibliography and Sourcelist.* Phoenix, AZ: Oryx.
32. Hennig, M., and Jardim, A. (1978) *The Managerial Women.* London: Marion Boyars.
33. Goffee, R., and Scase, R. (1985) *Women in Charge. The Experiences of Female Entrepreneurs.* London: Allen and Unwin.
34. McLane, H.S. (1980) *Selecting, Developing and Retaining Women Executives.* New York: Van Nostrand.

35. Jacklin, C.N., and Maccoby, E.E. (1975) "Sex Differences and Their Implications for Management." In E. Gordon and M. Strober (Eds.), *Bringing Women into Management*. New York: McGraw-Hill. pp. 23-38.
36. Meeker, B. F., and Weitzel-O' Neill, P.A. (1977) "Sex Roles and Interpersonal Behaviour in Task-orientat Groups." *American Sociological Review, 42* (1), 91-105.
37. Coyle, A. (1984) "Power Point." *The Guardian,* December 8.
38. Fogarty, M., Rapoport, R., and Rapoport, R.N. (1971) *Sex, Career and Family* London: Allen and Unwin.
39. Cooper, C., and Davidson, M.J. (1982) *High Pressure. Working Lives of Women Managers.* Glasgow: Fontana.
40. Marshall, J. (1984) *Women Managers. Travellers in a Male World.* Chichester: Wiley.
41. Davidson, M.J., and Cooper, C.L. (1983) *Stresss and the Woman Manager.* Oxford: Martin Robertson.
42. Davidson, M.J., and Cooper, C.L. (1984) "Occupational Stress in Female Managers. A Comparative Study." *Journal of Management Studies, 21(2)*
43. Davidson, M.J., and Cooper, C.L. (1984) "She Needs a Wife: Problems of Women Managers." *Leadership and Organization Development Journal, 5* (3), 1-30.
44. Donleavy, M.R. (1985) "Antidote to Babel: Organizational and Personal Renewal through Women and Men Working Together." *Management Education and Development, 16* (2), 230-37.
45. Fischer, M.L. (1985) "On Social Equality and Difference—A View from the Netherlands." *Management Education and Development, 16*(2), 201-10.
46. Whyte, W.F. (1949) "The Social Structure of the Restaurant." *American Journal of Sociology, 54,* 302-10.
47. Bass, B.M. (1981) *Stogdill's Handbook of Leadership. A Survey of Research.* New York: The Free Press.
48. Bartol, K. (1975) "The Effect of Male Versus Female Leaders on Follower Satisfaction and Performance." *Journal of Business Research, 3,* 31-42.
49. Bartol, K., and Wortman, M. (1975) "Male Versus Female Leaders: Effects on Perceived Leader Behaviour and Satisfaction in Hospitals." *Personnel Psychology, 28* (4), 533-47.
50. Mayes, S.S. (1979) "Women in Positions of Authority." *Signs: Journal of Women in Society and Culture, 4* (3), 556-68.
51. Marrett, C.M. (1972) "Centralization in Female Organizations: Reassessing the Evidence." *Social Problems, 19,* 348-57.
52. Grandjean, B.D., and Bernal. H.H. (1979) "Sex and Centralization in a Semi-profession." *Sociology of Work and Occupation, 6,* 84-102.
53. Sheriff, P., and Campbell, E.J. (1981) "La Place des Femmes: Un Dossier sur la Sociologie des Organizations." *Sociologie et Societes, 13,* 113-30.
54. Kanter, R.M. (1975) "The Impact of Hierarchical Structures on the Work Behavior of Women and Men." *Social Problems, 23,* 415-30.

55. Wells, T. (1973) "The Covert Power of Gender in Organization." *Journal of Contemporary Business, 2* (Summer), 53-68.
56. Korda, M. (1976) *Power!* London: Coronet.
57. Kanter, R.M. (1977) *Men and Women of the Corporation.* New York: Basic Books.
58. Korda, M. (1972) *Male Chauvinism! How It Works.* New York: Random House.
59. Vinnicombe, S. (1980) *Secretaries, Management and Organization.* London: Heinemann.
60. Eisenstein, Z.R. (Ed.), (1979) *Capitalist Patriarchy and the Case of Socialist Feminism.* Nfew York: Monthly Review Press.
61. Cockburn, C. (1983) *Brothers. Male Dominance and Technological Change.* London: Pluto.
62. Firestone, S. (1970) *The Dialectic of Sex: The Case of Feminist Revolution.* New York: Morrow.
63. Delphy, C. (as Dupont, C.) (1970) "Liberation des Femmes: Annee Zero." *Partisans,* No. 54-55. Reprinted as *The Main Enemy.* London: Women's Research and Resources Centre, 1977.
64. Delphy, C. (1984) *Close to Home. A Materialist Analysis of Women's Oppression.* London: Hutchinson.
65. Redstockings (1969) *Manifesto.* Quoted in A. Coote and B. Campbell (1982) *Sweet Freedom.* London: Blackwell.
66. Zetterberg, H.L. (1966) "The Secret Ranking." *Journal of Marriage and the Family, 28,* 134-42.
67. Bradford, D., Sargent, A., and Sprague, M. (1975) "Executive Man and Women: The Issue of Sexuality." In F. Gordon and M. Strober (Eds.). *Bringing Women into Management.* New York: McGraw-Hill.
68. Hearn, J., and Parkin, W. (1987) *"Sex" at "Work." The Power and Paradox of Organization Sexuality.* Brighton: Wheatsheaf; New York: St. Martin's.
69. Burrell, G. (1984) "Sex and Organizational Analysis." *organization Studies,* 5(2), 97-118.
70. Quinn, R. (1977) "Coping with Cupid: The Formation, Impact and Management of Romantic Relationship in Organizations." *Administrative Science Quarterly,* 22(1), 30-45.
71. MacKinnon, C. (1979) *The Sexual Harassment of Working Women.* New Haven: Yale University Press.
72. Rich, A. (1980) "Compulsory Heterosexuality and Lesbian Existence." *Signs: Journals of Women in Society and Culture,* 5(4), 631-60.
73. Tatchell, P. (1985) *Democratic Defence.* London: GMP.
74. Kentler, H. (1985) "Still Despised and Persecuted. On the Position of Homosexuals in the World of Work." *Planned Parenthood in Europe (Familienplanung in Europe),* 14(1), 32-35.
75. McIntosh, J. (1982) "Sexual Harassment. You Tell Us It's *Not* a Joke." *Cosmopolitan,* Óctober.

76. Leeds Trade Union and Community Resource and Information Centre (1983) *Sexual Harassment of Women at Work.* Leeds: TUCRIC.
77. Gutek, B.A., and Morasch, B. (1982) "Sex-Ratios, Sex-Role Spillover, and Sexual Harassment of Women at Work." *Journal of Social Issues. 38*(4) 55-74.
78. O'Brien, M. (1981) *The Politics of Reproduction.* London: Routledge and Kegan Paul.
79. Elshtain, J.B. (1981) *Public Man, Private Women.* Oxford: Martin Robertson.
80. Stacey, M., and Price, M. (1981) *Women, Power and Politics.* London: Tavistock.
81. Nowotny, H. (1981) "Women in Public Life in Austria." In C.F. Epstein and R.L. Coser (Eds.), *Access to Power Cross-national Studies of Women and Elites.* London. Allen and Unwin. pp. 147-56.
82. Skard, T., with Hernes, H. (1981) "Progress for Women: Increased Female Representation in Political Elites in Norway," In C.F. Epstein and R.L. Coser (Eds.), *Access to Power. Cross-national Studies of Women and Elites.* London: Allen and Unwin. pp. 76-89.
83. O'Brien, M. (1978) "The Dialectics of Reproduction." *Women's Studies International Quarterly, 1*(3), 233-39.
84. Stacey, M. (1981) "The Division of Labour Revisited or Overcoming the Two Adams." In P. Abrams, R. Deem, J. Finch, and P. Rock (Eds.), *Practice and Progress. British Sociology 1950-1980.* London: Allen and Unwin. pp. 172-90.
85. Gordon, L. (1975) "The Politics of Birth Control, 1920-1940. The Impact of Professionals." *International Journals of Health Services, 5*(2), 253-77.
86. Hanmer, J. (1977) "Community Action, Women's Aid and the Women's Liberation Movement." In M. Mayo (Ed.), *Women in the Community.* London: Routledge and Kegan Paul. pp. 91-108.
87. Hearn. J. (1982) "Notes on Patriarchy, Professionalization and the Semi-professions." *Sociology, 16*(2), 184-202.
88. Cohen, G. (1979) "Symbiotic Relations: Male Decision-makers and Female Support Groups in Britain and the United States." *Women's Studies International Quarterly,* 2(4), 391-406.
89. Cole, J., and Brintnall, D. (1975) "The Decline of a Babysitting Co-operative in a Non-co-operative Americaan Economy." *Urban Life and Culture.* 3(4), 456-63.
90. Joynt, P. (1983) *Cross Cultural Management.* Oslo: Norwegian School of Management.
91. Klykken, A.J., Klepper, U., and Joynt P. (1982) *Presence and Potential of Women in Management.* Oslo: Norwegian School of Management.
92. Hisrich, R.D. (1984) "The Women Entrepreneur in the United States and Puerto Rico: A Comparative Study." *Leadership and Organization Development Journal, 5* (5), 3-8.
93. Rohlen, T.P. (1974) *For Harmony and Strength. Japanese White-collar Organization in Anthropological Perspective.* Berkeley. CA: University of California Press.

94. Trevor, M. (1983) Japan's Reluctant Multinationals. London: Frances Pimer.
95. Silver, C.B. (1981) "Public Bureaucracy and Private Enterprise in the U.S. and France: Contexts for the Attainment of Executive Positions by Women." In C.F. Epstein and R.L. Coser (Eds.), *Access to Power. Cross-national Studies of Women and Elites.* London: Allen and Unwin. pp. 219-36.
96. Whitley, R. (1981) "Women, Business Schools and the Social Reproduction of Business Elites." In C.F. Epstein and R.L. Coser (Eds.), *Access to Power. Cross-national Stuidies of Women and Elites.* London: Allen and Unwin. pp. 185-92.
97. Epstein, C.F., and Coser, R.L. (Eds.) (1981) *Access to Power. Cross-national Studies of Women and Elites.* London: Allen and Unwin.
98. Lovenduski, J., and Hills, J. (Eds.) (1981) *The Politics of the Second Electorate.* London: Routledge and Kegan Paul.
99. Siltanen, J., and Stanworth, M. (Eds.) (1984) *Women and the Public Sphere. A Critique of Sociology and Politics.* London: Hutchinson.
100. Albrektsen, B.H. (1977) *Kvinner og Politisk Deltakelse* [Women and Political Participation]. Oslo: Pax. Cited by T. Skard, with H. Hernes (1981) "Progress for Women: Increased Female Representation in Political Elites in Norway.

Index